A BIRD BOOK
FOR THE POCKET

CONJUGI
ADJUTRICI
OPTIMÆ

A

BIRD BOOK

FOR THE POCKET

*Treating of all the regular British species,
with coloured plates to scale and an
illustrated chapter on eggs*

BY

EDMUND SANDARS

THIRD EDITION

OXFORD UNIVERSITY PRESS
LONDON: HUMPHREY MILFORD

OXFORD UNIVERSITY PRESS
AMEN HOUSE, E.C. 4
LONDON EDINBURGH GLASGOW
NEW YORK TORONTO MELBOURNE
CAPETOWN BOMBAY CALCUTTA
MADRAS
HUMPHREY MILFORD
PUBLISHER TO THE
UNIVERSITY

FIRST PRINTED	1927
SECOND EDITION	1929
THIRD EDITION	1933
SECOND IMPRESSION	1936
THIRD IMPRESSION	1939
FOURTH IMPRESSION	1942
FIFTH IMPRESSION	1943
SIXTH IMPRESSION	1945

PREFACE TO THIRD EDITION

THIS book has been brought up to date in the light of later knowledge and the most recent vagaries of scientific nomenclature have been followed. For brevity, I have retained the term "United Kingdom" in its obsolete sense, meaning Great Britain and Ireland.

The book is limited to our regular species, residents or migrants. Where recent research has divided a species into two (as in the case of the British and Continental Redbreasts), I have relegated one of them to a note. I have omitted a few very rare birds (*e.g.*, the Ortolan), although modern watchers have found their visits to be regular. My test is, does a sight of the bird produce a letter to the press ?

In my drawings a just general effect has been aimed at rather than feather accuracy. Unless otherwise stated, the plates show the cock bird in full mating plumage, and any variations of sex or season are described verbally. Where it has been easier to add a second drawing than to describe the plumage, I have done so.

The drawings are to scale. Small birds are given at half the natural size, large birds at one-fifth, and the book is divided accordingly. This division is, of course, not scientific, nor have I followed it strictly. To avoid separating families I have, in several cases, put a large bird with his smaller brethren, and drawn him to their scale, and *vice versa*. Some of the large birds are too large to be shewn on the one-fifth scale, and for these I have drawn a part of the bird at that scale and reproduced him, inset, smaller.

For the Latin names I feel that the value of standardization outweighs habit or taste, and I have decided to bow to the B.O.U. I have made only one innovation. Where their list duplicates or triplicates a name, I have ventured to square or cube it. Thus the poor little Wren, instead of being called *Troglodytes troglodytes troglodytes* (!), is called *Troglodytes*³. The Bullfinch becomes *Pyrrula*² *nesa*, instead of *Pyrrula pyrrula nesa;* the Barn Owl *Asio otus*², instead of *Asio otus otus;* and the father of all tame Geese *Anser*², in lieu of *Anser anser.*

By the order and by the English names that they have adopted I do not feel equally bound, and while, in deference, I call the Thrush *Turdus ericetorum*², I do not call it the "British Song Thrush." I call it the Thrush. Where there is an English name in common trivial use I feel strongly that with such one should not tamper. I therefore retain the much-criticised Hedge Sparrow as such ; and to one plea I remain unrepentantly obdurate, I will not drop the Stormy Petrel's "y." The popular names of our birds should be above pedantry and Lord Eldon was not called "the Storm-Petrel."

To shorten the book I have not described the plumage of immature birds or the materials and form of the nests. The date (in brackets) after the word "Nests" is the date of laying, and where the word "Lays" is used instead of "Nests," it means that no nest is made. I have not described nesting habits in the case of birds who nest abroad.

The Introduction consists of general remarks upon the structure, plumage, migration, and some of the habits of our birds, and

PREFACE

at the end of the book there is a chapter on eggs and an Index. I think that a single picture of one egg for each bird is often misleading, and I am sure that verbal descriptions are nearly useless. Measurements can only be averages. Nothing but access to a large collection can, in the case of some birds, teach one to know their eggs. In dealing with the subject, I have tried to make an Egg Sorter which will help in tracing the family, and in many cases the bird, to which an egg belongs. The Index contains, in small type, a number of local or alternative names not included in the text, and also, in italics, a glossary of such words as seem to need explanation.

To the would-be bird watcher I offer the following advice :—
Use an old-fashioned opera-glass, or a prismatic glass of low power (magnifying three to five times only) and with a large aperture, rather than the ordinary field-glass. Where you have to make a movement, such as raising your glasses, make it with the utmost slowness.

To those who wish to preserve our heritage of birds, I suggest that the offering of money for eggs or skins does more harm than a hard winter.

I do not claim to have added to existing knowledge. I have tried to give in the smallest possible bulk the greatest number of facts about each of our birds and a just picture of their beautiful forms and colouring.

EDMUND SANDARS.

January, 1933.

LIST OF CONTENTS AND CLASSIFICATION

THE SMALL BIRDS, *pp.* 2-86.

OF THE BIRDS BY ORDERS AND FAMILIES

THE LARGE BIRDS, *pp.* 90-230.

INTRODUCTION

THESE remarks relate only to the regular British Birds included in this book, and not to species which visit us irregularly as vagrants, or to domesticated birds, or imported strangers in parks or on ornamental waters.

All birds are hot-blooded, feathered, vertebrate bipeds, and all our birds are capable of flight.

THE WING.—Very little can here be said of anatomy. The skeleton of a bird is much like that of a man. The arm of a bird has become a wing by being lengthened and so adapted as to fold up Z-wise, retaining freedom of movement at the shoulder, but (once extended) having little or no other movement, remaining rigid like the blade of an oar. The fingers of the hand are reduced in number to three. One (the thumb) is very small, while the third is fused with the second. From them grow the large flight quills (primaries), and the rest of the main flight feathers (secondaries) spring from the forearm.

The vertebræ of the back are consolidated into a rigid block and the breast-bone is enlarged and endowed with a strong keel to support the powerful flight muscles.

THE BEAK.—Having devoted the arms to flight, birds use the beak as a hand. Very little use is made of the feet for this purpose. The Owls and Hawks kill with them, and the Owls use them to carry food to the mouth, as do the Shrikes (which kill with the beak), while many birds hold their food under the feet while eating, but apart from this, the bill has to serve all the uses of a hand, in eating, building, fighting or the toilet. To this end the neck is more flexible than that of any other vertebrate (it has from 10 to 15 vertebræ while a Giraffe has but 7), and the shape of the bones is such as to make a bird alone able to turn its head completely round to the back. The skull is developed forwards towards a beak which varies greatly in shape and is adapted to the bird's mode of life.

Thus, those which tear flesh have a markedly hooked beak, and, usually, a curved or indented edge which takes the place of teeth. (No bird has teeth.) Such are the Owls, Hawks, Cormorants, Sawbill Ducks, Skuas and Petrels. In a lesser degree, the Shrike, Cuckoo, Gannet, the Gulls, Rails, Pigeons and Game Birds have hooked beaks. There is a slight downward curve and a definite tooth edge to the beaks of the Thrushes; and the Warblers, Flycatchers and Crows have the downward curve.

There is a conical, wedge-shaped, powerful bill typical of the birds whose business is pecking wood, and of some of the divers; *e.g.*, the Nuthatch, Kingfisher, the Woodpeckers, Terns, Divers and Grebes. Those of the Herons, who spear, may be put in the same class.

Again, there is a seed or kernel cracking bill, broadened at the base, straight and sharp at the point. Such are those of the Tits and Finches which contrast markedly with the delicate, pointed beaks of the insect eating Warblers, Pipits, and Larks.

The Swallows, the Swift and Nightjar have, for insect capture on the wing, a remarkably wide gape with a side fringe of bristles to prevent the escape of their prey. The Gannet's long bill has also a wide gape for the similar trade of fishing.

The whole Goose order (Geese, Swans and Ducks) except the Sawbills, living as they do largely by sifting water for minute organisms, have a flattish, sensitive bill with comb-like edges for sifting and a hard nail-like point for more serious work.

The Waders (Snipe, Plovers and shore birds) are the family which vary most in the trades they ply and in the matter of bill. Their beaks are usually flexible and sensitive, with narrow gape, and vary greatly in length and curve.

The saw edge for gripping, as distinct from the toothed edge for chewing, belongs to the Sawbills and Herons.

The Nightjar and the Petrels have tubular nostrils.

Lastly, there are some strange forms which are not easily classified; the Tree Creeper, Crossbill, Chough, Razorbill, Puffin and Coot.

INTRODUCTION

THE LEGS.—Of a bird's legs it should be noted that the bone which is our thigh is always short and enclosed in the skin of the body. The bird usually stands on its toes, and moves by bending the knee joint and the ankle joint. This latter, being the only visible bend in the leg, is usually called the "knee" of the bird, and the part from it to the ball of the foot (called the "tarsus") is a long shank enclosed in scaly skin.

THE TOES.—In regard to their toes the birds may be grouped as follows :—

Three toes only, all pointing forwards : the Stone Curlew, Sanderling, Golden, Ringed and Kentish Plovers, Dotterel, Oyster Catcher, Kittiwake and the Auks.

Three toes forward and a small raised "dew-claw" behind : the Geese, Swans and Ducks, Petrels, Divers and Game Birds, and of the Waders, the Common and Purple Sandpipers, Ruff, Godwit, Redshank, Greenshank, Grey Plover, Lapwing and Turnstone.

Four toes all forward : the Swift, Nightjar, Cormorants and Gannet.

Four toes, two fore and two aft : the Woodpeckers, the Cuckoo and the Owls. In the case of the Owls the outer hind toe can go forward.

Four toes, three forward (of which the inner two are united in one sheath until the last joint) and one behind : the Kingfisher.

All other birds have three toes forward and one behind.

As to webbed feet : partly webbed, the toes more or less united by membranes at their bases, are common to the Heron, Stone Curlew, nearly all the Waders and the Game Birds. Broad webs on the separate toes mark the Red-Necked Phalarope, the Coot and the Grebes.

Fully webbed feet, all the forward toes united, belong to the Geese, Swans, Ducks, Cormorants, Gannet, Gulls, Auks, Petrels and Divers, and, in addition, the Diving Ducks have lobes to the hind toes.

INTRODUCTION

THE LUNGS.—Birds are enabled to maintain their blood temperature (which is higher than that of any animal) by reason of two things, their superb breathing apparatus, which oxygenates the blood more effectively than any other, and their feather covering, which retains the heat.

Oddly enough, the lungs of a bird are relatively very small. But behind them are large sack-like air cavities extending throughout the body and many times larger than the lungs themselves. The lungs are, as it were, placed in the throat of a large bellows. Further, these sacks are inflated and compressed by the muscles which work the wings. Thus the bellows are automatically blown in flight. This system of air sacks is extended to fill the bones of most birds in place of marrow, so that the frame of the bird is of the strongest and lightest tubular construction. The extent of such aeration of the bones varies greatly in the different species, being greatest in the large, powerful flyers and least in the smaller birds and some of the sea-birds.*

MOULTING.—All birds moult every feather at least once a year. To prevent interference with flight, most birds moult slowly, shedding the feathers in orderly rotation. The few exceptions to this rule, the quick moulters, are water birds or those which fly little,—the Geese, the male Ducks, the Auks, the Divers, and the Corncrake. Those which depend entirely upon flight for their living are often very slow moulters ; thus most of the Hawks moult almost all the year, the Swallow family, Swift and Nightjar for seven months, the Gulls five to seven months, and the Pigeons six months.

The general rule, then, is that every bird has a complete autumn moult, of varying duration, beginning about July or August, and in time for the migrants to be new-feathered for the southward flight. Apart from the Goose Order, which is dealt with separately later, the following are the only exceptions :— The long-continued moult of most of the Hawks cannot be ascribed to any special season. The Puffin's autumn moult is not complete, but confined to the body feathers. Some of the

---

* NOTE.—Much in the Eagle, and Gannet ; little or none in the Swift, Swallow, Gulls, Cormorants and Divers.

migrants which leave us early interrupt their moult after shedding the body feathers here and either continue it, or begin again and complete it, abroad during the winter. These are the Spotted Flycatcher, Shrike, Swallow, Martins, Swift, Nightjar, Cuckoo and Turtle Dove.

In addition to the autumn moult, some birds moult in the spring. This spring moult may be partial or complete. It is partial, extending only to the head and neck or upper body, in the case of a few birds.* A larger number shed all the feathers of the body, and in most cases the inner wing feathers and a part of the tail.§ The spring moult is complete in the case of most of the Warblers,† the Wryneck, Little Stint, the Terns, the Puffin and the Divers. Some few feathers are also shed in the spring by the Chaffinch, the Woodpeckers, the Long-Eared Owl, Moorhen and Coot.

The cocks of the Capercaillie, Black Cock, Grouse, and Partridge have a partial (summer) moult of head and neck just after the breeding season, when they put on eclipse dress for a month or so before the complete autumn moult.

The Ptarmigan moults the body in the spring, moults again completely in the late summer, and yet again the body in the autumn ; so that the process is continuous from March to December and shews three distinct plumages.

Of all the moults that of the Goose Order is the most complicated and there are yet some gaps in our knowledge of the facts. The Geese have the usual autumn moult, beginning with the quills all together ; all but the Grey Lag moult the head and body again in spring. The Swans seem to be as the Grey Lag. The Sheldrake moults all but the back in the summer, and the

---

* Note.—*Viz.*, the Snow, Cirl and Reed Buntings, the Gannet, Woodcock, Lapwing and Quail, and the hens of the Grouse and Partridge.

Note.—*Viz.*, the Mistle Thrush, Wheatear, Whinchat, Lesser Whitethroat, Blackcap, Chiffchaff, the Wagtails and Pipits, the Pied Flycatcher, Merlin, Kestrel (?), Cormorant, Shag, Stone Curlew, the whole of the Wader family (except the Woodcock, Lapwing and Little Stint), the Gulls, Skuas, the Razorbill, the Guillemots, all the Grebes, the Corncrake, Spotted Crake and Water Rail.

† Note.—*Viz.*, the Whitethroat, Garden, Willow, Wood, Grasshopper Sedge and Reed Warblers.

body again in the autumn. The Goldeneye moults the body in the autumn and all except the rump and underparts in the summer. The two Scoters moult (completely ?) in the autumn, the body again through the winter, and the head and neck yet again in the spring. In all the other Ducks there is a difference between the sexes. The females have the usual autumn moult, effected slowly, and also, in the spring, a moult extending to the body and often the tail. The Drakes have their complete moult in the summer, beginning, in some cases as early as May, as soon as the eggs are hatched. This is a swift moult, preventing flight and producing the " eclipse " dress. They then have a second moult of the body (and usually the tail) in autumn.*

COLOUR CHANGES.—Care must be taken to distinguish between a moult and a marked change of colour in the plumage. There may be a moult without such change, as that of the Sheldrake or those of the female Ducks ; and there may be marked changes of colour without moult, either by the bird wearing off parts of the feathers as do the Starling and most of the Finches, or by changes of pigment which alter the colour of feathers without their being shed, as in the case of the Black-Headed Gull.

There are very marked seasonal changes of plumage for both sexes in the case of most of the Waders and the Ptarmigan. The Starling has a marked seasonal change due to the rubbing off of the buff tips of the feathers which, by the spring, makes them appear uniformly dark.

SEX DIFFERENCES.—There is little or no visible difference between the sexes in the Heron, Bittern, Stone Curlew and all the Waders, Rails, Doves, or in any of the fully web-footed birds except the Ducks. There is also no such difference in the case of about one-half of the species of the Perching Birds (e.g., the Redbreast, the Tree Sparrow, and the Martins). The most marked differences appear in the Ducks and Game Birds.

---

* NOTE.—The above is the general rule. There are some variations. Thus the Ducks of the Mallard and Widgeon continue the autumn moult until the spring moult begins. Both sexes of the Long-Tailed Duck seem to show signs of three distinct moults. The Duck of the Eider has a prolonged body moult, and sheds the quills together (as do the Scoter Ducks) like the Drakes. It seems doubtful whether the females of the Sawbills have any spring moult.

Where there is a difference, the hen, whose period of brooding exposes her to danger, is usually the smaller and less conspicuous bird. The female Red-Necked Phalarope and sometimes the Dotterel are the only more brilliant birds, but the Hawks, the Owls, and the Whimbrel have females larger than the males— see, notably, the Peregrine. Where there is no distinction, and the colouring is conspicuous, it will often be found that the birds build in holes or covered nests. Often the most distinctive part of the male's dress is assumed for the mating season only— *e.g.*, the Ruff.

MIGRATION.—The general rule is that our birds have a yearly movement from south (winter) to north (summer), and breed in the summer at the northern extremity of their beats. The shape and climate of Europe gives a west to east trend to these movements, as well as south to north. There are three main exits from our islands to the colder (summer) resorts, namely, (1) N.E. to Norway and the Arctic coasts (the birds leave from any part of our coasts from the Humber to the Shetlands); (2) E. to the Dutch coast for the Baltic and central Europe (the birds leave from the S.E. coasts); and (3) N.W. to Iceland and Greenland (the birds leave from the Shetlands). The exits to the warmer (winter) resorts are across the Channel, but mainly near the western and eastern ends, to Brittany and the mouth of the Rhine respectively. In the main, the same routes are used for entrance as for exit. Most birds on long journeys seem to prefer to follow the coast lines or large rivers.

RESIDENTS :—*i.e.*, species which are found here all the year round. Almost all these species include many individual birds which migrate, leaving us for the summer or winter, and many include birds which are here only on passage.*

NON-MIGRANTS : The following are exceptions to the general rule in that they have little or no range of movement :—Dartford Warbler, Dippers, Nuthatch, all our Tits, Shetland and St. Kilda

---

* NOTE.—Individual birds belonging to all four classes (residents, summer, winter, and passage, migrants) are found among each of the following species :—Mistle Thrush, Blackbird, Meadow Pipit, Skylark, Greenfinch, Linnet, Lesser Redpoll, Starling, Teal, Woodcock, Snipe, Dunlin, Curlew, Redshank, Lapwing, Oyster Catcher, Common and Black-Headed Gulls.

INTRODUCTION

Wrens, Tree Creeper, Bullfinch, Sparrow, Scottish Crossbill, Cirl Bunting, all our Woodpeckers, Chough, Magpie, our Jay, Barn-, Tawny- and Little- Owls, Golden Eagle, Mute Swan, Rock Dove and all the Game Birds except the Quail.

SUMMER MIGRANTS to the United Kingdom : The following is a list of our summer migrants somewhat in the order in which they appear :—

March : Lesser Black-Backed Gull[W], Wheatear, Chiffchaff[W], Ring Ouzel[W], Sand Martin, Willow Warbler[W].

April : Swallow, Wryneck, Garganey, Blackcap, Common Sandpiper[W], Tree Pipit, Yellow and Blue-headed Wagtails, Cuckoo, Stone Curlew[W], Martin, Greenshank[W], Redstart, Whitethroat, Nightingale, Montagu's Harrier, Common and Little Terns, Kentish Plover, Whinchat, Wood-, Sedge- and Reed- Warblers, Lesser Whitethroat, the Crakes[W], Grasshopper- and Garden- Warblers, Pied Flycatcher, Sandwich Tern, Turtle Dove, Swift, Nightjar, Spotted Flycatcher, Hobby, Dotterel.

May and June : Shrike, Quail, Phalarope, Arctic and Roseate Terns, Marsh Warbler.

All these summer migrants, except the Reed- and Marsh-Warblers, Nightjar, Montagu's Harrier, Hobby, Stone Curlew and Quail, also breed in colder lands than ours and are therefore also here on passage.

WINTER MIGRANTS to the United Kingdom, in the same order :

July and August : Crossbill[b], Lapland Dunlin, Purple Sandpiper, N. Golden Plover.

September : Cont. Thrush, Widgeon[b], Slavonian Grebe[b], Scoter[b], Snow Bunting[b], Scaup[b], Jack Snipe, Velvet Scoter, Goldeneye, Gt. N. Diver, Barnacle and Pink-Footed Geese, Cont. Hedge Sparrow, Brent Goose, Red- and Black[b]-necked Grebes, Cont. Redbreast, N. Spotted Woodpecker, Redwing, Cont. Goldcrest, Long-tailed Duck[b], Short-eared Owl[b], White-fronted Goose.

October-November : Brambling[b], Bean Goose, Fieldfare, Smew, Mealy Redpoll, Whooper[b] and Bewick's Swans.

W NOTE.—These species include birds which sometimes winter with us.
b NOTE.—These species sometimes breed, or have recently bred, with us.

All these winter migrants, except the N. Spotted Woodpecker, have wintered (and almost all habitually winter) in warmer countries and are therefore also here on passage. There is not much evidence about the Goose Order, and the Pink-Footed Goose, Long-Tailed Duck, Smew and Swans are only occasionally found south of us.

BIRDS OF PASSAGE, *i.e.*, passing through the United Kingdom in spring, autumn, or both, but wintering south, and summering north, of us. The following are so classified here :—

> Greenland Wheatear, Scandinavian and Siberian Chiffchaffs, N. Willow Warbler, Cont. Great Tit, White Wagtail[b], Great Snipe, Knot[w], Sanderling[w], Little Stint, Green-[w] Wood-[w] and Curlew- Sandpipers, Ruff[b], Bar-Tailed Godwit[ws], Whimbrel[bs], Grey Plover[w], Turnstone[w], Scandinavian Lesser Black-Backed Gull[w], Black Tern, White-Tailed Eagle[b], Osprey[b].

NESTS.—The following birds make little or no attempt to build a nest: the Nightjar, the Waders, Terns, the Razorbill, the Guillemots, Divers and Game Birds. The Barn-, Tawny- and Little Owls and, usually, the Stock Dove, find a hole. The following find a hole and build a nest in it : the true Tits (*Paridæ*) except the Long-Tailed, the Starling, Jackdaw and Sheldrake. The following make a hole : the Woodpeckers, the Kingfisher, Puffin, and the Petrels ; while the Sand Martin also makes a loose nest in the hole it has made. The Nuthatch finds a hole and often plasters up the entrance with mud until it is the right size. Other users of mud in the nest are the Mistle Thrush, Thrush, Blackbird, Ring Ouzel, Swallow and Martin. The skilfully-built nest, cup or dome, belongs to the Perching Birds alone ; all others make a rough platform or mound only. The Tits, Owls and Kestrel will steal holes, and those of Rabbits are used by the Tawny Owl, Sheldrake, Puffin and Stock Dove and, often, the Little Owl. The Cuckoo is purely parasitic.

---

w NOTE.—These species include birds which sometimes winter with us.

b NOTE.—These species sometimes breed, or have recently bred, with us.

s NOTE.—Non-breeding individuals often stay the summer.

INTRODUCTION

FOOD.—As a general rule, all birds eat a mixed animal and vegetable diet. The food of the young tends to be less vegetable. The following eat no vegetable food : the Swallows, the Swift, the Owls and Hawks, the Cormorant and Shag. Mainly vegetarian are the Finches, Geese, Pigeons and Game Birds.

VOICE.—The birds having a real song (swan fable to the contrary notwithstanding) all belong to the small Perching Birds. The following notes apply only to these.

SONGSTERS.—The following birds are usually heard to sing :
all the year : MistleThrush, Redbreast, Hedge Sparrow, Dipper, Wren, Goldfinch, Starling, and the Larks ;
in spring and summer : (residents), Thrush, Greenfinch, Linnet and Yellow Hammer ; and (migrants), Whinchat, Willow, Sedge and Reed Warblers and Swallow ;
by night as well as day : Nightingale and Sedge Warbler, and (sometimes) the Thrush and Wood Lark ;
in flight : (habitually) the Wren, Wood and Reed Warblers, all Pipits and Larks, Greenfinch, Siskin and Goldfinch, and (sometimes) the Blackbird and Swallow.

GAIT.—All birds walk except the Perching Birds who hop. Of these the Wagtails, Pipits, Larks, Starling and Crows walk, and the Thrushes sometimes run. The Starling and Rook will hop if hurried. The Crossbill uses the beak in climbing ; the Tree Creeper and Woodpeckers (not the Wryneck or Nuthatch) the tail. In swimming, the general rule is alternate foot strokes when on the surface and simultaneous when under water. The Auks and the Dabchick swim under water with the wings.

FLIGHT.—Generally speaking the rapidity of the wing beats varies with the size (particularly the length) of the wing in relation to the weight of the bird—the smaller the wing the more rapid the beat. Sailing intervals are common to both the big-winged birds (notably the Gannet, Buzzard, Gulls, and Swift) ; and to the small-winged (the Starling and the Game Birds). Intervals with closed wings mark the flight of the Perching Birds, notably the Linnets, Finches, Thrushes and Swallows. The Kestrel and the Terns remain stationary, hovering, and also, sometimes, the Kingfisher, Shrike, Sparrow and Skylark.

In flight, the Perching Birds and the Woodpeckers hold up their legs; the Buntings, the Corncrake and Moorhen (when flushed) and the Petrels, hang their legs downwards. All others stretch them out behind.

HABITS.—*Roosting:* Most birds tuck the head "under the wing" in sleep; not the Owls or the Grebes. The Game Birds sit down; many of the others stand, often on one leg. The Tits, Wren, Martins, Swift, Owls, Petrels and Pigeons roost in the nest.

The Bearded Tit and the Game Birds are scratchers of the ground. The Larks, Sparrows and Game Birds are frequent dust bathers.

Birds differ greatly in the degree to which the young are developed at the time they are hatched.

They are hatched helpless in the case of all the Perching Birds, Woodpeckers, the Wryneck, Swift, Kingfisher, Cuckoo, the Owls, Hawks, Cormorants, the Gannet, Heron, Bittern, the Petrels and Pigeons. Such young are called "nidicolous"; they are found, usually, but not always, in nests in trees or on cliffs, where precocious wandering might be fatal; are hatched after a short period of incubation from relatively small eggs, the yolk of which is exhausted before the chick is born, and they are blind and naked, or with a scanty down. They need long brooding and feeding by the parents.

Those most active and soon out of the nest (" nidifugous ") are the whole Goose Order, the Waders, Divers, Grebes and, to a lesser degree, the Gulls, Terns, Auks and Rails and the Nightjar. These active chicks, soon able to fend for themselves, are always found in nests on or near the ground; they are produced after longer incubation, from relatively large eggs and retain a part of the yolk in their bodies which helps to bridge over the short time before they can feed themselves. They are all hatched open-eyed and down-clad, and although some are fed by the parents for a short time, this is hardly necessary.

In most cases the care of the young falls mainly upon the female, sometimes entirely (*e.g.*, the Game Birds, except the Partridge, and the Ducks, but not the Geese or Swans), never exclusively upon the male, except in the doubtful case of the Red-Necked Phalarope. The Pigeons divide the work evenly between the sexes.

PART I

THE
SMALL BIRDS

NAMELY
THE PERCHING BIRDS EXCEPT THE CROWS,
AND ALSO
THE WOODPECKERS, SWIFT,
NIGHTJAR AND KINGFISHER

DRAWN TO ONE-HALF NATURAL SIZE

MISTLE THRUSH—*TURDUS VISCIVORUS.*[2]

Length 11 ins. *Sexes* alike. *Resident* throughout United Kingdom, rarer northwards. Also winter, and some summer, migrants. Open fields and hedge timber, parks, orchards, gardens. *Nests* (Feb.-Apr.) in forks of trees, often near houses; in default, in rock ledges; 4-5 eggs, 1-2 broods. Cock helps build, incubate and feed. *Food:* All berries, fruit, worms, snails, insects. *Voice:* Fine, low and varied song, chiefly in autumn and winter. "Storm cock." Cry: A harsh rattle. *Flight:* Swift, strong, undulating, jerky. *Gait:* Hops; rapid, jerky movements with erect pauses. *Manners:* Bold with birds, shy of men. "Listens" for worms. Hammers snails. Begin to pack end of June, big flocks by autumn, but flying scattered. Flocks break up in mid-winter. When disturbed, rise successively in a line.

MISTLE THRUSH

THRUSH—*TURDUS ERICETORUM.*[2]

Length 8½ ins. *Sexes* alike. *Resident* throughout United Kingdom, with large summer migration. Gardens, hedgerows, woods, meadows and plough. *Nests* (March-April) in thick bushes, ivy or banks; 4-5 eggs, 2 or 3 broods. Cock helps build and feeds. *Food :* Snails, insects, worms, berries, fruit, shell-fish. *Voice :* Fine, varied, cheerful song, containing a phrase like "Did he do it?" repeated twice or thrice, March to July, and again in autumn, all day till dark, delivered from perch. Alarm cry, "Tcheek, Tcheek!" and "Ptick!" Roosts noisily. *Flight :* Strong, undulating, jerky. *Gait :* Hops and runs. *Manners :* Hides from man, "listens" for worms, hammers snails. Migrates at night, alone. Never packs. Young feed later broods. Shams sick to decoy from nest. Dances in courting.

> NOTE.—The Continental type (*T. e. philomelos*), also found in United Kingdom as winter migrant and passage, is slightly paler; and the resident Hebridean variety (*T. e. hebridensis*) is darker.

THRUSH

REDWING—*TURDUS MUSICUS.*[2]

Length 8½ ins. *Sexes* alike. *Winter migrant* and passage September-May throughout United Kingdom. *Nests* abroad. *Food :* Insects, small snails and (in frost) berries and even roots. *Voice :* No song in United Kingdom ; subdued, whispering alarm note. *Flight :* When disturbed, fly to trees and thence, singly, on again. *Gait :* Hops. *Manners :* Always in flocks and seldom near houses, otherwise similar to Thrush. Night migrant, returning to same places yearly. The most delicate of the Thrushes, dying in hard winters.

N.B.—The strong red only shews when wing is lifted.

REDWING

FIELDFARE—*TURDUS PILARIS.*

Length 10 ins. *Hen* somewhat duller. *Winter migrant* from October-April and passage. Generally distributed, in open country, plough and pasture, throughout the United Kingdom. *Nests* abroad. *Food :* Insects, snails, worms and (in frost) berries. *Voice :* No song in the United Kingdom. Cry of " Uch Chu Chu Chut ! " *Flight :* Wheeling, before settling. *Gait :* Hops. *Manners :* All face same way when feeding or perching. Migrates at night. Gregarious and always wandering. Very noisy when roosting.

FIELDFARE

BLACKBIRD—*TURDUS MERULA*.[2]

Length 10 ins. *Hen* shewn in plate, not to scale. *Resident*, except in extreme north; also, throughout United Kingdom, winter migrant and passage. Gardens, hedgerow, shrubbery, woodside. *Nests* (March) in bushes, evergreens and hedges; 4-5 eggs, 2-4 broods. Cock helps build and feeds. *Food:* Snails, worms, insects, berries and, largely, fruit. *Voice:* Song, early and late, mellow, leisurely, delivered from perch, or sometimes in flight between perches, repeated at brief intervals, often spoiled by a squeak at the end, from January to end of July. When startled, cackling cry. Metallic cry before roosting, "Tcheek! Mink!" *Flight:* Low, strong, cocking tail on alighting. *Gait:* Hops and runs. *Manners:* Very shy when breeding. Cock quarrelsome. Young feed later broods. "Listens" for worms, hammers snails. Duels during courtship; sings during fights. Will feign sick to decoy from nest.

BLACKBIRD
(Cock and Hen)

RING OUZEL—*TURDUS TORQUATUS.*[2]

Length 10 ins. *Hen* lighter and browner, gorget duller and narrower. *Summer migrant* March-Sept., in wild hill country throughout United Kingdom, also passage. *Nests* (end April) in heather, niche in rock, bank or stone wall; 4 eggs, 2 broods. Cock helps build and feeds. *Food :* Worms, snails (broken), fruits, berries. *Voice :* Song during breeding season, wild and glad. Cry, like Blackbird. *Flight :* Cocks tail on alighting. *Gait :* Hops and stands on ground. *Manners :* Very bold if nesting, will attack intruders and "tumble" to decoy them away, with sharp alarm note. Gestures like Blackbird's. Complicated courtship dances of both sexes.

RING OUZEL

WHEATEAR—*ŒNANTHE*.[3]

Length 6 ins. *Hen* has dark brown ear coverts, upper parts brown and under parts buff, shewn in plate, not to scale. In autumn, cock resembles hen. *Summer migrant* early March-October. Downs, warrens and mountains, on arable only in autumn. *Nests* (mid-April) in rabbit-holes, stone walls, peat stacks ; 4-7 eggs, 2 broods. *Food :* Larvæ, spiders, insects (caught flying). *Voice :* Very slight song, April-June. Cry of "Chack Chack." Imitative powers. *Flight :* Short, low, flits from stone to stone. *Gait :* Perches on stone or clod, dips head and flirts tail, hops fast. *Manners :* Packs on S. Downs for migration, never otherwise. Cock sings flying in courtship. Wheatear means "white rump."

NOTE —The slightly larger Greenland Wheatear (*Œ² leucorboa*) occurs in passage.

REDSTART—*PHŒNICURUS*.[3]

Length 5½ ins. *Hen* shewn in plate. Both sexes greyer in autumn. *Summer migrant* and passage, mid-April-September in E. and S. United Kingdom only. Rather rare. Orchards, gardens, old walls, woods. Cocks come first and peg out claims. *Nests* (early May) hollow trees, holes, boxes ; 6 eggs, 1 brood. Cock feeds, does not incubate. *Food :* Flies, insects (taken flying), spiders. The young eat caterpillars. *Voice :* Slight warble from high perch, April-June. Alarm cry, "Wheet !" *Flight :* Short, hovering. *Manners :* Found in arable on migration. Perches conspicuously, spreads and shivers orange tail. Redstart means "red tail."

WHEATEAR
(Cock and Hen)

REDSTART
(Cock and Hen)

WHINCHAT—*SAXICOLA RUBETRA.*[2]

Length 5 ins. *Hen* duller, white wing-spot smaller, breast spotted. In autumn cock duller. *Summer migrant*, mid April-Oct. General through Great Britain, mainly E., rarer in Ireland. Pastures and commons, plough during migration. *Nests* (May) on ground in furze or thick grass ; 5-6 eggs, 1 brood. Cock feeds. *Food :* Beetles, flies, insects, worms, molluscs. *Voice :* Sings pleasantly on wing or low twig, fanning tail, April to mid-June. Call, "U-tick !" *Flight :* Low and hurried, hovering over weeds to feed. *Manners :* Roosts on the ground. Perches on stone, clod, wire, rail or post, taking insects on the wing. All movements abrupt and alert.

STONECHAT—*SAXICOLA TORQUATA HIBER-NANS.*

Length 5 ins. *Hen* shewn in plate. In autumn, cock paler beneath, upper feathers margined red. *Resident* generally in United Kingdom, migrating from N. to S. Local and erratic. Open commons and furze. *Nests* (early April) in grass or broken ground below bushes ; 5-6 eggs, 2 broods. Cock feeds, does not incubate. *Food :* Small moths, butterflies, insects, worms, beetles, few seeds. *Voice :* Song short and pleasing, early April-June. Scolding note, "H-wit Jur Jur !" *Flight :* Low and rapid. *Manners :* Restless, constantly jerking tail, perching on top twig or wire, takes insects on the wing. Anxious when nest is approached, flits from bush to bush " cursing."

WHINCHAT

STONECHAT
(Cock and Hen)

REDBREAST—*ERITHACUS RUBECULA MELO-PHILUS.*

Length 5¾ ins. *Sexes* alike. *Resident* throughout United Kingdom; also summer migrants. Gardens, hedges, banks. *Nests* (end March) in hedge-banks, holes, ivy, pots; 5-7 eggs, 2-3 broods. Cock feeds the young. *Food :* Insects, worms, berries and fruit. *Voice :* Fine song throughout year. Various call notes. *Flight :* Hovers over insects in air or water. *Gait :* Hops. *Manners :* Saucy, fiercely pugnacious, particularly among themselves. Each pair holds a defined estate. Quick, alert movements. Perches on branch or post, bobs head and flirts tail. Takes insects in air from perch. Love displays of puffings and swayings. In winter, hen has separate estate and sings.

Note.—The Continental type (*E. r.²*), paler in breast, is also seen as winter migrant and passage.

NIGHTINGALE—*LUSCINIA MEGARHYNCHA.²*

Length 6½ ins. *Sexes* alike. *Summer migrant*, mid-April to Sept. Generally in S. and E. England. Cocks come first and young leave in August. Small woods and coppices near water, commons. *Nests* (early May) on ground in low undergrowth on sunny side; 4-5 eggs, 1 brood. Cock helps build and feeds young. *Food :* Worms, insects, ants' eggs, fruit and berries. Young eat spiders, ants and caterpillars. *Voice :* Cock has fine song till June, day and night, in good weather. Later, a croak. Call, "Wate Wate, Cur Cur!" *Flight :* Short. *Gait :* Hops. *Manners :* Return to same places yearly. Alert movements much like Robin, but greater dignity. When disturbed nesting, the parents flit from bough to bough, calling.

18

REDBREAST
(Adult and Young)

NIGHTINGALE

WHITETHROAT—*SYLVIA COMMUNIS*.[2]

Length 5½ ins. *Hen* without pink on breast, head brown. *Summer migrant* late April-Sept., young leave last. Common all over United Kingdom, except N. Scotland. Nettles and gardens. *Nests* (May) in nettles, weeds or brambles under hedges; 4-5 eggs, 1 brood. *Food:* Small caterpillars, insects and, autumn, soft fruits. *Voice:* Hurried and vehement song, except in August, from perch, with excited, jerky gestures, short flights and erected crest, "aerial dance." Call, " Churr ! " Alarm, " Tec ! " *Gait:* Creeps up thickets. *Manners:* In courtship brings hen a piece of grass. Very restless, twisting, tip-toeing, puffing out throat. Sings when approached. Cock begins nest, helps incubate and feed. If young threatened, feigns lameness.

LESSER WHITETHROAT—*SYLVIA CURRUCA*.[2]

Length 5¼ ins. *Sexes* alike. *Summer migrant* (mid-April-Sept.) chiefly S. and E. England. Rarer than above. Orchards, gardens, thick copse. *Nests* (early May) in dense, tall hedges, low bushes and brambles; 4-6 eggs, 1 brood. *Food:* Insects, larvæ, soft fruit, berries. *Flight:* Undulating rapid beats. *Voice:* Song, 2 or 3 unmusical notes, following a low crooning warble, puffing out throat, usually in tree. Notes like Whitethroat. *Manners:* Moves incessantly. Perches higher than Whitethroat; shyer, skulking. Cocks, on first arrival, travel over large areas in high trees. Cocks help build, incubate and feed. When feeding young, birds cling upside-down on a twig.

WHITETHROAT

LESSER WHITETHROAT

BLACKCAP—*SYLVIA ATRICAPILLA.*[2]

Length 5¾ ins. *Hen :* Cap, bright red-brown and remainder browner. *Summer migrant* April-Sept., also passage. Rare in England, rarer in Scotland and Ireland. Woods, orchards, gardens, commons, furze. *Nests* (May) in low bushes ; 4-5 eggs, 1-2 broods. Cock helps build, incubate and feed. *Food :* Insects (taken on wing), soft berries. *Voice :* Very fine song, ringing, animated. Delivered on spray, throat and crest puffed out, from arrival till end July. Alarm, " Tack Tack ! " *Manners :* In courtship cock brings hen piece of grass. Restless, very shy, silent if approached. Combative in protecting estate.

GARDEN WARBLER—*SYLVIA BORIN.*

Length 5½ ins. *Sexes* alike. *Summer migrant* May to end Sept., and passage. Local and sparse in Great Britain. Very rare in Ireland. Commonest in Lincolnshire. Woods and orchards. *Nests* (May-June) in low thorny bushes, peas ; 4-5 eggs, 1 brood. Cock helps incubate, feed and build nest. *Food :* Insects, peas, fruit and berries. Young eat insects and caterpillars. *Voice :* Song, soft long warbling from arrival to mid-July, sometimes at twilight. Call, " Tec ! " Alarm, a plaintive " Bit, Bit, Bit ! " *Gait :* Hops, sometimes up trees. *Manners :* Generally resembles Blackcap. These two species resent each other's presence.

BLACKCAP

GARDEN WARBLER

CHIFFCHAFF—*PHYLLOSCOPUS COLLYBITA.*[2]

Length 4¾ ins. *Sexes* alike. *Summer migrant* late Mar. to Oct., also some few residents. General all over United Kingdom, mainly S. and W. *Nests* (May) off ground in ferns or rank grass ; 6 eggs, 1 or 2 broods. Cock does not build or incubate, but feeds. *Food :* Insects and few berries. *Voice :* Song, " Chiff Chaff !" all summer and all day, from high tree-tops. *Gait :* Seldom on ground. Creeps, searching small twigs. *Manners :* Cocks come first and peg out claims. Fight to defend them. Pugnacious. Frequent high trees, incessantly feeding. Leaf hunting. Mimic courtship combats.

> NOTE.—The slightly larger, paler Scandinavian Chiffchaff (*Ph. c. abietinus*) occurs in passage, and a smaller, greyer Siberian variety (*Ph. c. tristis*) is a regular autumn visitor to the Isles.

WILLOW WARBLER—*PHYLLOSCOPUS TROCHILUS.*[2]

Length 5 ins. *Sexes* alike. In autumn, yellower. *Summer migrant*, early April to mid-Sept. ; also a few residents and passage. General and very abundant throughout United Kingdom. Woods, copses, orchards, gardens, commons. *Nests* (Apr.-May) in long grass, below a bush, or in wall ; 6-7 eggs, 1-2 broods. *Food :* Flies, aphides ; in autumn, few berries. *Voice :* Song, throughout stay, merry, repetitive, descending, diminishing. Call," Whit" and "Tuí." *Gait :* Hops, creeps searching twigs. *Manners :* Trustful of man, anxious only if nest approached, restless, graceful, stooping. Sometimes takes flies on wing. Pugnacious. In autumn, chases Tits. No connection with willows.

> NOTE.—A greyer form, the Northern Willow Warbler (*Ph. t. eversmanni*), occurs in passage.

CHIFFCHAFF

WILLOW WARBLER

WOOD WARBLER—*PHYLLOSCOPUS SIBILAT-RIX*.[2]

Length 5¼ ins. *Sexes* alike. *Summer migrant* (mid-April-Sept.), throughout Great Britain, rare in Ireland. Woods, particularly oak and beech. Local. *Food :* Flies (taken on wing), other insects, berries in autumn. *Nests* (May) on ground in dead bracken on hill-side or hollows ; 6-7 eggs, 1 brood. Cock helps build and feeds. *Voice :* Song, April to early July, few clear notes, hurrying to close, "shivering" wings and tail. Calls "Dee-ur Dee-ur Dee-ur !," "Tui !" and "Ting !" *Flight :* Hovers to pick food from under leaves, then back to perch, searching on and on. *Manners :* Frequents high trees, flitting from tree to tree, singing in flight. Hen sits close.

GRASSHOPPER WARBLER—*LOCUSTELLA NÆVIA*.[2]

Length 5½ ins. *Sexes* alike. *Summer migrant* (end April-Sept.). General throughout United Kingdom, commonest Northumbria, rarer Scotland. Returns yearly to old haunts. Fens, reclaimed lands, heaths, coarse hedgerows. *Food :* Insects. *Nests* (May) in clumps of dry grass, 4-7 eggs, 1 or 2 broods. Hen broods, cock helps feed. *Voice :* Rapid trilling, chirping song—"Reeler"—early and late, from top twig or reed, delivered with open mouth and thrilling body. Alarm note, "Tic Tic Tac !" *Flight :* Hen, flushed, flies with drooping, outspread, round tail. *Gait :* Runs and creeps, mouse-like. *Manners :* Skulks in low growth. Flies to cover on slightest alarm. Migrates in flocks.

WOOD WARBLER

GRASSHOPPER WARBLER

SEDGE WARBLER—*ACROCEPHALUS SCHŒ-NOBÆNUS.*

Length 4¾ ins. *Sexes* alike. *Summer migrant* late April to end Sept. and passage. Cocks arrive first. Common throughout United Kingdom. Waterside, also copses and hedgerows. *Nests* (May) in lower branches of willow or rank herbage, hollow in ground or bushes ; 5-6 eggs, 1 brood. Cock does not build but feeds. *Food :* Aquatic insects, slugs, worms, larvæ and elderberries in autumn. *Voice :* Constant gabbling hurried and mixed song, from thick reeds, day and night in summer. Sings from a particular perch. Imitates cries of other birds. *Flight :* Low, hurried, muttering. *Gait :* Clings sideways to reeds. *Manners :* Very restless, constantly moving from reed to reed, rarely on tops. Will allow approach. Sings when alarmed. Combative. In autumn, in standing wheat.

REED WARBLER—*ACROCEPHALUS SCIR-PACEUS.*[2]

Length 5½ ins. *Sexes* alike. *Summer migrant* (May-Sept.). Fairly common in S. and E. and mid-England, wherever reeds are abundant. Cocks arrive first. *Nests* (June) are slung on 4 reeds ; 4-5 eggs, 1 brood. Cock does not build or incubate, but feeds. *Food :* Aquatic insects and larvæ, spiders, slugs, worms, fruit and berries. *Voice :* Song, May to mid-July and Sept., low chiding, and high musical notes, hurried as he flits in reeds. *Manners :* Like those of the Sedge Warbler, except that he is more limited to the waterside.

NOTE.—The Marsh Warbler (*A. palustris*), an almost identical bird, breeds in a few southern counties. It is slightly paler, differs in song, stays only from June to August, and the nest hangs from " handles."

SEDGE WARBLER

REED WARBLER

DARTFORD WARBLER—*MELIZOPHILUS UNDATUS DARTFORDIENSIS.*

Length 5 ins. *Hen* rather smaller, paler and browner. *Resident* in S. England in varying districts. Very local and rare. Extinct in Kent. Furze bushes, commons. *Nests* (May) low in thick furze and heather; 3-5 eggs, 2 broods. *Food:* Insects; in autumn, soft berries. *Voice:* Song jerky, given with antic jumps. Cry, "Pit Tiu!" Alarm, "Cha Cha!" *Flight:* Quick, short dips, alights abruptly, spreading tail. *Gait:* Creeps. *Manners:* Restless, skulking and hard to see except in spring when, singing, he bounces up from top of tree like a shuttle-cock. Parents lure away from nest by tumbling. Crest erectile.

GOLDCREST—*REGULUS² ANGLORUM.*

Length 3½ ins. *Hen* duller with black streaks below pale yellow crest. *Resident* (but rare after winter of 1916) throughout United Kingdom; also, irregularly, winter migrants in large flocks, Sept.-April. In conifers, particularly yews. *Nests* (April) beneath end of branch. Cock helps build and feed, does not incubate; 7-12 eggs, 2 broods. *Food:* Insects. *Voice:* Cock's song, weak and thin, delivered while feeding, almost incessant Feb.-Oct. *Flight:* Hovering love dance with chirps. Fly-catching. *Gait:* Hops along branches, hanging upside-down. *Manners:* Restless and keeps to deep shadows. Not shy, very sociable. Flocks with Tits and Creepers. Hen sits close. In flocks, except when breeding. Crest erectile.

NOTE.—The Continental type (R.³), the migrant, has greyer nape of neck.

DARTFORD WARBLER

GOLDCREST

HEDGE SPARROW—*PRUNELLA MODULARIS OCCIDENTALIS.*

Length 5¾ ins. *Sexes* alike. *Resident* throughout United Kingdom. Hedgerows and gardens. *Nests:* (April) among evergreens, hedgerows, stick heaps; 4-5 eggs, 2-3 broods. Cock helps feed. *Food:* Insects, spiders and seeds; in hard winters, crumbs. *Voice:* Song, all the year in fine weather, chiefly spring, from hedge top; 2 notes, in hurried succession, forming a trill. Also a plaintive, piping call note. *Flight:* Short. *Gait:* Hops with one foot forward, seeking food on ground. *Manners:* Excitable, fidgety, " Shufflewing." Mock combats in courtship. Hardy.

> NOTE.—The Continental type (*P.m.*²), winter migrant, has paler breast.

DIPPER—*CINCLUS*² *GULARIS.*

Length 7 ins. *Sexes* alike. *Resident* in all hilly districts of United Kingdom, descending in hard winters. Rapid streams. *Nests* (March-April) by streams, on rock, wall, bridge, tree or culvert; 4-6 eggs, 2-3 broods. Cock helps build, incubate and feed. Old nests are sometimes used. *Food:* Insects, chiefly aquatic, spiders, crustaceans, molluscs (regurgitating pellets), rarely fry, not ova. *Voice:* Short song all year, chiefly winter and spring, day and night. Call, " Chit Chit ! " *Flight:* Low, with whirring wings. *Gait:* Walks and runs, scrambles, sometimes hops on grass. *Manners:* Perches on boulder, curtseys, jerks his tail. Walks into and under water. Swims on surface and dives. Washes beak. Seldom leaves his beat, pugnaciously defended. Sings in fights.

> NOTE.—The Irish variety (*C.*² *hibernicus*) has a narrower chestnut belt.

HEDGE SPARROW

DIPPER

NUTHATCH—*SITTA EUROPÆA AFFINIS.*

Length 5½ ins. *Sexes* alike. *Resident*, central and S.E.
England and Wales, rare in Scotland. Local. Parks,
woodland, old timber, orchards. *Nests* (April) in
natural holes or Woodpecker's borings, filled with
mud to right size—" Mudstopper"; 5-8 eggs,
1-2 broods. Cock helps build and feed, not incubate.
Food: Minute insects and larvæ; later, nuts and
acorns. *Voice*: Song, Feb.-May, "Tui Tui Tui!"
low mellow call note, "Be quick! Be quick!"
Flight: In courtship, flies to a height and then
swoops down with outstretched wings. *Gait*:
Climbs up, down and across trunks and branches in
short, jerky, sidelong runs. *Manners*: Do not pack.
Trustful of man, fights other birds. Splits nuts in
cracks. Said to roost head downwards.

BEARDED TIT—*PANURUS BIARMICUS.*[2]

Length 6¼ ins. *Hen*, no blue on head, no black
moustache. *Resident* in Norfolk Broads. *Nests*
(April) on edge of reed-bed, close to water; 5-7 eggs,
2-3 broods. Cock helps build, incubate and feed.
Food: Insects, larvæ, molluscs. *Voice*: Call note,
"Ping Ping!" Scolding, "P'whut!" *Gait*:
Twisting and climbing round and up reeds, straddling.
Flight: Laboured, undulating, slow, with outspread
twisting tail. *Manners*: Never leaves reeds. Hates
wind. In autumn they pack in flocks of 20 to 40, but
do not leave area. Packs break up for spring. Cocks
fight fiercely. In courtship, tail erected and beard
puffed out; joint nuptial flight high into air, "dropping like stones."

NUTHATCH

BEARDED TIT

LONG-TAILED TIT—*ÆGITHALOS CAUDATUS ROSEUS.*

Length 5½ ins. *Sexes* alike. *Resident* throughout U.K., rare in Scotland. Woods and plantations. *Nests* (April) in thick thorn, holly, furze, ivy or lichen-clad high branches; 6-12 eggs, 1-2 broods. Cock builds and feeds. Return to old nesting sites. *Food:* Insects and larvæ. *Voice:* Call, shrill "Zee Zee Tchup!" *Flight:* Swift, arrow-like. *Gait:* Every form of acrobatic trick. *Manners:* Restless, sociable, not shy, ever feeding. Hen sits with tail bent back over head. Both roost in nest when breeding. Young stay with parents till next spring. Packs with other Tits and small birds in winter, wandering in tree-tops, not far-feeding, and roosting in clumps. Impatiently hurry on ahead of others.

GREAT TIT—*PARUS MAJOR NEWTONI.*

Length 5¾ ins. *Sexes* alike. *Resident* throughout U.K., except extreme N. Woods, plantations, orchards and shrubberies. *Nests* (end April) in holes and cavities; also old Rook's, Crow's or Pie's nests; 5-11 eggs; 1, rarely 2, broods. Cock does not incubate, feeds. *Voice:* Spring "song" (mid-Aug. to mid-June), two powerful, metallic notes, "Tea Cher!" The "Saw-sharpener." *Food:* Insects, nuts, conifer seeds, corn, carrion. Omnivorous. Splits hard nuts. *Flight:* Laboured, fluttering. *Gait:* Seldom on ground, hops and creeps all over trees. *Manners:* Active, restless, resolute, strong, bold in defence of its nest. Hen sits close. Pretty acrobatic gestures. Less gregarious than the other Tits, but joins in winter bands.

NOTE.—The Continental type with slenderer bill (*P. m.*[2]) is seen on passage. In some years abundant.

LONG-TAILED TIT

GREAT TIT

COAL TIT—*PARUS ATER BRITANNICUS.*

Length 4½ ins. *Hen* slightly duller. *Resident* through-out United Kingdom. Woods, chiefly conifer. *Nests* (April) low in old stump or hole in hedge-bottom or wall ; 7-11 eggs, 1 brood. Cock does not build. *Food :* Chiefly insects ; in autumn, nuts and conifer seeds. Omnivorous. *Voice :* As Great Tit, but shriller. *Flight, Gait and Manners :* Generally as all other Tits, but even more active and goes more to ground to feed.

> NOTE.—The Irish variety (P. *a. hibernicus*) has yellow instead of white on cheeks and neck.

MARSH TIT—*PARUS PALUSTRIS DRESSERI.*

Length 4½ ins. *Sexes* alike. *Resident* England and Wales, local and rather scarce save in Kent and Pembroke. Woods, groves, hedgerows, orchards, gardens. *Nests* (April-May) in natural holes, slightly enlarged, in stumps and trees ; 5-9 eggs, 1-2 broods. *Food :* Insects ; later, berries, beech-mast, nuts, larch and thistle seeds. *Voice :* Song, Jan.-May (and sporadically all through year, except Aug. and Sept.), similar to Great Tit only not so loud. *Flight, Gait and Manners :* Like those of Coal Tit. The name is misleading.

> NOTE.—A similar bird, found locally throughout England and in Scotland, has lately been given specific rank as the Willow Tit (P. *atricapillus kleinschmidti*). It has a dull sooty brown head.

COAL TIT

MARSH TIT

BLUE TIT—*PARUS CÆRULEUS OBSCURUS.*

Length 4¼ ins. *Sexes* alike. *Resident* and common throughout United Kingdom. *Nests* (end April) in small hole in tree or wall, boxes, etc. Returns to same nest; 7-12 eggs, 1 brood. Cock helps build, incubate and feed. *Food :* Chiefly insects in spring ; nuts, acorns, larch seeds later. Crumbs in winter. Omnivorous. *Voice :* Song, mid-Aug. to mid-June, like Great Tit, but not quite so loud, followed by a rippling tinkle. Also " Zee Zee Zee ! " *Flight, Gait and Manners :* Like those of the Great Tit. Hen sits close and hisses if disturbed.

CRESTED TIT—*PARUS CRISTATUS SCOTICUS.*

Length 4½ ins. *Hen* slightly shorter crest and less black on throat. *Resident,* very local, in pine forests of Scotland (Spey Valley). *Nests* (April) in hole of decayed pine or other tree; 5-6 eggs, 1 brood. *Food :* Insects and larvæ, small seeds and berries. *Voice :* No song. Call note, sharp, piercing. *Flight, Gait and Manners :* Like those of other Tits. Packs with them and other small birds.

BLUE TIT

CRESTED TIT

WREN—*TROGLODYTES*.[3]

Length 3½ ins. *Sexes* alike. *Resident* and omnipresent in United Kingdom. In all hedges and thick undergrowth. *Nests* (end April) in trees, bushes, holes, crevices, banks; 5-6, up to 16, eggs; 2 broods. Cock builds spare nests, helps incubate and feeds. *Food:* Minute insects, rarely fruit and seeds. *Voice:* Loud, clear, high, trilling song all the year and in all weathers. *Flight:* Wings whirr audibly. *Gait:* Hops and climbs. *Manners:* Secretive, never tame or unsuspicious. Restlessly flitting, climbing and feeding. Will forsake if nest is disturbed. Has been seen to walk into water after food.

> NOTE.—The Shetland variety (*T.*[2] *zetlandicus*) is darker, and St. Kilda bird (*T.*[2] *hirtensis*) lighter. Both these varieties are distinctly larger than *T*[3]. The Outer Hebridean Wren (*T*[2] *hebridensis*) is also darker but no larger.

TREE CREEPER—*CERTHIA FAMILIARIS BRITTANICA*.

Length 5 ins. *Sexes* alike. *Resident* throughout the U.K. in well-wooded districts. *Nests* (end April) behind loose bark of tree, or in ivy, or in crevice of wall; 5-7 eggs, 1-2 broods. Cock helps build, incubate and feed. *Food:* Minute bark insects. *Voice:* Song, all year, chiefly in spring, 3 or 4 feebly shrill notes. Call note and alarm, shrill, high, "Zit!" *Gait:* Mouselike, creeping, hops. *Flight:* Swooping. *Manners:* Solitary. Seldom leaves woods. Endless, minute, laborious peering and feeding, working in zigzags up the bole, then, with a short querulous note, dropping slantwise to the foot of another tree and up again. In autumn and winter, individuals go with the Tits and Goldcrests. Hen sits close and hisses if disturbed. Cannot bear hard winter.

WREN

TREE CREEPER

WATER WAGTAIL—*MOTACILLA ALBA YARRELLII.*

Length 7½ ins. In winter, white chin and throat and greyer back. *Hen* has greyer back and shorter tail. *Resident*, widespread; also summer migrants (early March-Sept.). Lawns and pasture near streams. *Nests* (April) in hollow in ground or hole in bank or rock. 4-6 eggs, 2-3 broods. Cock helps build and feed. *Food:* Chiefly insects. *Voice:* Song, spring and autumn, low warbling. Usual note, double chirp, " Tizit ! " *Flight:* Curving, dipping, erratic; spreads tail. *Gait:* Walks, runs, wags tail up and down. *Manners:* Impulsive. Stands, runs, wags tail, flies after insects, stands, flies a short way, stands, wags tail, etc. Follows cattle. In courtship, hovers down and struts, displaying wing and neck. Roosts in reed bed.

> Note.—Similar Continental White Wagtail (*M. a.*[2]), shewn in plate, common in passage, is greyer. Said sometimes to roost in trees. Has nested in U.K.

GREY WAGTAIL—*MOTACILLA CINEREA.*[2]

Length 7½ ins. In winter, black of throat is white. *Hen*, shorter tail, head and back greener, throat mostly white. *Resident* throughout United Kingdom in hilly country, very rarely on low lands of S. and E. England. Internal migrations. Chiefly mountain streams. *Nests* (end Apl.) on ground in herbage or under bush or rock; 4-6 eggs, 1-2 broods. *Food:* Insects, small crustacea and fish fry. *Voice:* Spring song, sweet, swallow-like. Note like *Alba.* *Flight, Gait and Manners:* Like *Alba.* Stays closer to water. Even more graceful and volatile. The rarest native Wagtail.

WATER WAGTAIL

GREY WAGTAIL

YELLOW WAGTAIL—*MOTACILLA FLAVA RAYI.*

Length 6½ ins.   *Hen* duller and smaller.   In autumn, both paler.   *Summer migrant*, end March-Sept., local in England, rare in the W., in Scotland and Ireland; also passage.   Downs, pastures, commons, arable. Not restricted to waterside till autumn.   Never near houses.   Males come first.   *Nests* (late May) under grass or corn; 4-7 eggs, 1-2 broods.   Cock does not incubate, helps feed.   *Food:* Insects and molluscs. *Voice:* No song.   Call, two shrill notes.   *Flight, Gait and Manners:* Like Water Wagtail.   Follows the plough.   In courtship, cock hovers over hen.

NOTE.—The Continental type Blue-headed Wagtail (*M. f.²*), with white chin and blue-grey head, is also seen in the United Kingdom and has bred here.

MEADOW PIPIT—*ANTHUS PRATENSIS.*

Length 5¾ ins.   *Sexes* alike.   *Resident* throughout United Kingdom; also winter migrants and passage. Waste lands.   Moves S. in winter.   The commonest Pipit.   *Nests* (end April) in small cavity under grass or ling; 4-6 eggs, 2 broods.   *Food:* Insects, caterpillars and seeds.   *Voice:* Song, April-July, series of metallic, monotonous, pleasant notes.   Soars up to 40 feet and glides down with tail spread and wings half-closed, motionless, singing.   Rarely sings on ground.   Alarm, sharp plaintive chirp.   *Flight:* Hurried, jerky.   *Gait:* Runs and walks, wags tail sedately.   *Manners:* Seeks food on ground.   Timid, but reluctant to fly.   Has gamey scent.   In courtship, cock stands on low bush or stone whence to rise for song.   Anxious if nest approached.

YELLOW WAGTAIL

MEADOW PIPIT

TREE PIPIT—*ANTHUS TRIVIALIS*.[2]

Length 6 ins. *Sexes* alike. *Summer migrant*, end Apl.
to end Sept., and passage. General in Great Britain,
except W. Cornwall and N. Scotland. Most wood-
sides and big trees in pastures. *Nests* (end May) near
the perching tree, in well covered hollow in the
ground; 4-6 eggs, 1 brood. Cock feeds, but does
not seem to build or incubate. *Voice :* Song,
variable, sometimes like canary, delivered sailing
down in spirals from height of 40 odd feet and
continued on favourite perch in lower tone. (April to
mid-July). *Flight :* Laborious, long fluttering leaps,
steadier in autumn. *Food, Gait and Feeding Habits :*
Like Meadow Pipit. *Manners :* Cocks, on arrival,
choose feeding ground and song tree, and hold
estates till autumn against others. Before leaving
(gregariously) they resort to the stubbles in small
packs.

ROCK PIPIT—*ANTHUS SPINOLETTA PETROSUS*

Length 6½ ins. *Sexes* alike. *Resident* throughout
United Kingdom on cliff and rock; sea-coasts only.
Also summer migrants. *Nests* (April-May) on the
ground, carefully hidden in rocks; 4-5 eggs, 2 broods.
Food : Minute crustaceans, marine insects and worms.
In autumn, seeds. *Voice :* Song and delivery as
Meadow Pipit. *Gait, Flight and Manners :* As Meadow
Pipit. In autumn and winter packs in very small
packs and resorts to salt marshes and low grounds.
Sometimes wades.

TREE PIPIT

ROCK PIPIT

SKYLARK—*ALAUDA ARVENSIS.*[2]

Length 7¾ ins. *Sexes* alike. After autumn moult, more tawny. *Resident* throughout United Kingdom. Also large summer and winter migrations and internal movements. All open land, preferably arable. *Nests* (April) in hollow in ground; 3-5 eggs, 2-3 broods. Cock brings materials and feeds, but does not incubate. *Food :* Worms, insects, spiders and, later, seeds, turnip leaves, etc. *Voice :* Song (end Jan. to end July, and Sept. to Nov.) profuse, unpremeditated art, delivered soaring almost vertically to 1,000 feet, with pauses, changing tone when sailing down. Sometimes sings from ground. *Flight :* Powerful, quick beating, showing long pointed wing and white edgings to tail. *Gait :* Runs, hops only in courtship. *Manners :* Jealous and combative. Very anxious if nest approached, crouch for concealment. Said to have gamey scent when running (not sitting). Begin to flock in Sept. Feeds and roosts on ground; dust bather.

WOOD LARK—*LULLULA ARBOREA.*[2]

Length 5½ ins. *Sexes* alike. After autumn moult redder. *Resident* in England, Wales and a few places in Ireland. Very local. Internal winter moves southwards. Resembles the Skylark in all respects except the following :—*Nests* under a bush. *Voice :* Song less powerful and varied, but even more constant. He ascends and descends in spirals, does not rise so high. Also sings on a tree-perch and rises thence. Sings more commonly on ground. *Manners :* Has a favourite perch for sitting and singing.

SKYLARK

WOOD LARK

SPOTTED FLYCATCHER—*MUSCICAPA STRIATA.*[2]

Length 5¾ ins. *Sexes alike.* *Summer migrant*, mid-May to mid-Sept. throughout United Kingdom, rarer northwards. Parks, gardens, orchards and hedges. *Nests* (June) in ivy or trees, on, or against, walls; 4-6 eggs, 1 brood, rarely 2. Cock builds and feeds, but does not incubate. Return to old nest. *Voice :* Rare, rambling song May and June. Feeble chirp 2 or 3 times repeated. *Food :* Insects, chiefly flies. *Flight, Gait and Manners :* Sits all the time on certain favourite perches in a defined area, dashes out to snap (audibly) insects and returns to perch. Fearless, listless and depressed looking. Cock feeds hen who sits close.

PIED FLYCATCHER—*FICEDULA HYPOLEUCA.*[2]

Length 4¾ ins. *Hen* greyish brown instead of black, the white dingy, 3 side tail-feathers edged with black. In autumn, cock resembles hen. *Summer migrant*, end April to end Sept. Rare and local, N. England, Wales and S. Scotland. Commonest, Lakes and N. Wales. Also passage. Orchards and gardens. *Nests* (end May) in a hole of some kind, usually near stream; 6-8 eggs, 1 brood. Uses old nests. Cock feeds hen and young, does not usually incubate. Hen sits close. *Food :* Insects. *Voice :* Song, April to June, vivacious, spirited. Alarm notes : Cock, "Titatit ! " Hen, "Wiw Wit ! " *Flight, Gait and Manners :* Similar to Spotted, but well groomed and sprightly looking. More often feeds on ground. Not so skilful a fly catcher, nor so regular in returning to perch. Cocks fight before pairing and peg out claims.

SPOTTED FLYCATCHER

PIED FLYCATCHER

RED-BACKED SHRIKE—*LANIUS COLLURIO.*[2]

Length 7 ins. *Hen*, chestnut head, rump and tail. Buff chest laced black. *Summer migrant*, early May-Aug., mostly S. and E. Woods, gardens, marsh and common. Bushes. *Nests* (May) in hedgerows or brambles. Same site yearly; 5-7 eggs, 1 brood. Cock helps build and feed, does not incubate. *Food :* Small birds, lizards, mice, bees, beetles. *Voice :* Few shrill notes in May and June. *Flight :* Swooping. *Gait :* Hops. *Manners :* Sits alert on bush top, swoops on prey, plucks birds, impales on thorns. " Butcher Bird." In courtship, cock shakes and droops wings and feeds hen.

SWALLOW—*HIRUNDO RUSTICA.*[2]

Length 8 ins. *Hen*, less red on forehead, less black on breast, under parts white, tails shorter. *Summer migrant*, early April-end Sept., and passage, throughout United Kingdom. Villages and farms. *Nests* (May) in open saucer-shaped mud nest, lined, on level joists in barns. Return to old nests ; 4-6 eggs, 2 broods. Both build. Cock does not incubate, but feeds hen and young. *Food :* Insects. *Voice :* Cheerful, twittering song (April-Sept.), delivered from perch, sometimes on wing. Alarm, "Wheet Wheet ! " *Flight :* Very swift, circling, skimming. *Gait :* Walks, waddling. *Manners :* Gregarious in feeding, nesting and exercising. Almost always on wing wherever insects are. Will pursue Hawks. Follow cattle for flies. Drink and wash on wing. Pack in large flocks before leaving, perching on wires and roosting in osier-beds. First brood of young leave first.

RED-BACKED SHRIKE

SWALLOW

MARTIN—*DELICHON URBICA.*[2]

Length 5¼ ins. *Sexes* alike. *Summer migrant*, mid-April to mid-Oct., and passage throughout United Kingdom, rare in N. Scotland. *Nests* (May) half-cup of mud, with entrance hole, hanging under eaves, bridges, or ledges in cliffs; 4-5 eggs, 2-3 broods. Cock builds, incubates and feeds. *Food :* Insects. *Voice :* Song, all the time in United Kingdom, low guttural warbling. Delivered clinging to wall or nest edge. On the wing, a harsh guttural " Pri ! " *Flight :* As Swallow, but not quite so swift, graceful or quick at turning. *Gait :* Delicate walk as if picking his way, often with wing help. *Manners :* Similar to Swallow. More sociable when breeding. Does not wash on the wing. In the late summer they pack with Swallows and Sand Martins and roost in osiers.

SAND MARTIN—*RIPARIA.*[3]

Length 4¾ ins. *Hen* has a narrower band across chest. *Summer migrant*, early April to mid-Sept., throughout United Kingdom. Local in breeding. *Nests* (May) in holes or crevices in sea cliffs or sands, or clay banks near water. Railway cuttings, gravel pits. Returns to old holes. Both birds tunnel, in the morning. Cock feeds ; 4-6 eggs, 2 broods. *Flight :* Like Martin, but jerkier ; also hovering, moth-like, before holes. Much over water. *Voice :* Cock has low twittering song, hovering before hole. Low monotonous note when flying. Scream if alarmed. *Food, Gait and Manners :* As Martin, but never associating with man. On completion of breeding they swarm with Swallows and Martins.

MARTIN

SAND MARTIN

GREENFINCH—*CHLORIS.*[3]

Length 6 ins. *Hen* much browner, no bright yellow. Both browner in autumn. *Resident*, also large winter and some summer migration. Common throughout United Kingdom. Groves, gardens, hedgerows, trees, parks. *Nests* (May) among thick branches of bushes; 4-6 eggs, 2-3 broods. *Food :* Seeds and insects. Young fed on caterpillars and macerated weed seeds. *Voice :* Series of soft, melodious, warbled notes (Feb.-Aug.) delivered in air, flapping wings and circling down to perch; also low and long-drawn trill, "Poo-i !"; also a shocked scream. *Flight :* Undulating, wheels above roosting place in winter. *Gait :* Hops. *Manners :* Very sociable, in parties of 3-6 even when nesting. Not jealous or combative. In courtship, cock flies up and circles round singing and descends again into leaves. Roosts in evergreens. After summer they flock to fields and associate with Sparrows and Chaffinches, feeding on ground and trees.

SISKIN—*SPINUS.*[2]

Length 4½ ins. *Hen* duller, no black on head. Both greyer in autumn. *Resident* and winter migrant. Chiefly N. Scotland and Ireland, further S. in winter. Pine forests. *Nests* (April) in high pine or birch tree; 4-5 eggs, 2 broods. *Food :* Seeds, buds. Young : regurgitated seeds. *Voice :* Song, canary-like, delivered soaring above trees, with fluttering wings and out-spread tail and floating down. Call, small musical twittering. *Manners :* Tit-like attitudes in high twigs. Roosts in thick trees. In autumn flocks with Redpolls, Goldcrests and Tits, and migrates southwards to N. England.

GREENFINCH

SISKIN

HAWFINCH—*COCCOTHRAUSTES.*[3]

Length 7 ins. Bills change to pinky-yellow in winter. *Hen* paler and less red. *Resident* throughout Great Britain, chiefly in S.E. Dense woods, plantations and copses. *Nests* (end April) in tree or bush, particularly thorn; 4-6 eggs, 1 brood. Cock helps incubate and feed, and feeds hen. *Food:* Seeds, berries, kernels of cherries. Young: caterpillars and insects. *Voice:* Song, Feb.-June, sharp chattering noise. A short click when flying from bush to bush. *Flight:* Undulating, swift and strong. *Gait:* Hops. *Manners:* Very wary, vigilant and shy. Perches in tree-tops when away from lair and flies on seeing man. Roosts in tree-tops; in winter, in hedges. Seldom with other birds. In autumn, flocks.

BULLFINCH—*PYRRHULA*[2] *NESA.*

Length 6¾ ins. *Hen* shewn in plate not to scale. *Resident* throughout United Kingdom. Woods, plantations, thickets and undergrowth by streams. *Nests* (May) in holly, yew or dark thick bush; 4-5 eggs, 1-2 broods. Cock helps build, feed and incubate, and feeds hen. *Food:* Buds, fruit, seeds and some insects. Young: insects and regurgitated seeds. *Voice:* Song (both sexes) flute-like, soft, low, in breeding season and in winter. Hen sings from time when young can feed themselves till autumn moult. *Flight:* Undulating. *Gait:* Hops. *Manners:* Very exclusive. Pair for life and always together. Kiss. Family parties are seen during the winter.

HAWFINCH

BULLFINCH
(Cock and Hen)

GOLDFINCH—*CARDUELIS[2] BRITANNICA*.

Length 5 ins. *Sexes* alike. *Resident*, commoner S.; also summer migrants and passage. Frequents waste land, thistles. *Nests* (May) in fruit-trees or shrubs; 4-5 eggs, 2 broods. Cock helps build and feed, does not incubate. Feeds hen. *Food* : Seeds, chiefly of weeds, insects. Young : insects and regurgitated seeds. *Voice* : Lively, twittering song, all the year, on perch and wing. Musical call notes. *Flight* : Undulating from weed to weed. *Gait* : Hops. *Manners* : Roosts in tree-tops. Nuptial display of wings. In autumn flocks and wanders over waste lands.

CHAFFINCH—*FRINGILLA CŒLEBS*.[2]

Length 6½ ins. *Hen*, shewn in plate not to scale. *Resident* (except the Isles), winter migrants and passage. Hedgerow, garden, copse. *Nests* (April) in cleft of shrub or tree, or on level branch; 4-5 eggs, 1-2 broods. Cock helps build, incubate and feed. *Voice* : Song, mid-Feb. to June, rapid, gay, defiant, from prominent perch and soon repeated, bird erect and still. Call, "Pink Pink!" *Food* : Insects taken on ground and in air. *Flight* : Jerky, spreading tail. *Gait* : Hops. *Manners* : Jealous, pugnacious, anxious if nest approached. Feed much on roads. Roost in trees and bushes. Double nuptial flight. In autumn, migrant flocks of separate sexes.

GOLDFINCH

CHAFFINCH
(Cock and Hen)

SPARROW—*PASSER DOMESTICUS.*[2]

Length 6½ ins. *Hen* shewn in plate, not to scale. In winter cock's black becomes fainter and beak brown. *Resident* and omnipresent, wherever man is, in United Kingdom. *Nests* (April-May) in trees, ivy, rocks, spouts, eaves, any recess. Steals other birds' nests; 3-7 eggs, 2-4 broods. Cock helps build, incubate (?) and feed. *Food :* Seeds, buds, fruit, berries, insects, spiders, grain. Young: chiefly insects. *Voice :* Continuous, chattering chirp all the year. *Flight :* Quick beating, with intermittent sailing drops in descent, or when not hurried. Straight to destination. *Gait :* Hops. *Manners :* Quarrelsome, bold, fussy. Nuptial display of throat with drooping wings. Tears yellow flowers. Roosts noisily in winter in holes and other birds' nests; in summer, in trees and reed beds. Packs in autumn.

TREE SPARROW—*PASSER MONTANUS.*[2]

Length 5½ ins. *Sexes* alike. *Resident* and winter migrant throughout Great Britain, except extreme S.W.; in Ireland, only very local. *Nests* (May) in holes, trees, buildings, sandpits, cliffs; 4-6 eggs, 2-3 broods. Cock helps build, incubate and feed. *Food, Flight, Gait and Manners :* Similar to Sparrow, except that they are mostly country birds.

SPARROW
(Cock and Hen)

TREE SPARROW

BRAMBLING—*FRINGILLA MONTIFRINGILLA.*

Length 6 ins. Plate shews winter plumage. Nuptial dress has black head, white wing-bars and brighter chestnut. *Hen*, crown reddish-brown, feathers tipped grey; black streak over eye; cheeks and neck ash-grey; rest duller than cock. *Winter migrant*, Oct.-March, throughout United Kingdom, commonest between Forth and Humber. Beech woods. *Nests* abroad*. *Food :* In U.K., chiefly beech-mast and alder seeds ; later, insects. *Voice :* No song in U.K., lively chirruping. *Gait :* Hops. *Flight :* As Chaffinch. *Manners :* In U.K. always in flocks, often with Chaffinches, roosting in evergreens. Does not return to same place in successive years.

* N.B.—Has nested in United Kingdom.

LINNET—*ACANTHIS CANNABINA.*[2]

Length 5¾ ins. *Hen* duller and without crimson. Cocks lack crimson patch in winter and their plumage, generally, is very variable. *Resident* throughout United Kingdom, except Highlands. Summer and winter migrants and passage. Waste land, furze. *Nests* (April-May) in furze or other bush ; 4-6 eggs, 2-3 broods. Cock does not incubate, but feeds. *Food :* Seeds, berries, insects, buds, fruit. Young : regurgitated seeds. *Voice :* Song, gentle canary-like trill in spring, delivered in flight. Continual twittering. *Flight :* High, swift, suddenly checking and darting off in new direction or dropping suddenly. *Gait :* Hops. *Manners :* Graceful, very sociable. In small flocks of 3-6 even in spring. Sometimes roosts on ground (only Finch to do this). In autumn and winter, flocks, travels much, chattering before roosting.

BRAMBLING

LINNET

LESSER REDPOLL—*ACANTHIS FLAMMEA CABARET.*

Length 4½ ins. *Hen* duller, no red on breast. In autumn, cock resembles hen and both have yellow beaks. *Resident* throughout U.K. Scarce in S.W. Local, chiefly in the N. Birch woods, fir plantations, shrubberies. *Nests* (May) trees, bushes, hedges, furze; 4-6 eggs, 1-2 broods. *Food:* In summer, insects from higher branches; winter, seeds on the ground. *Voice, Flight and Gait:* Like Linnet. *Manners:* Lively, graceful, very acrobatic. Flock after breeding. Packs augment in autumn. Sometimes associate with Tits, Goldcrests and Siskins.

NOTE.—The Continental, Mealy Redpoll (*A. f.*[2]), winter migrant, is slightly larger and paler.

TWITE—*ACANTHIS FLAVIROSTRIS.*[2]

Length 5¼ ins. *Hen*, no red on rump, which is striated. *Resident* Scotland and N. and mid-England and Ireland, commoner northwards. Winter migrants. Moves to S. England in winter. Mountains and moors. *Nests* (May) under or in heather, gorse, bushes, or rabbit-holes; 5-6 eggs, 2 broods. Cock helps build and feed. *Food:* Seeds. *Voice, Flight, Gait and Manners:* Like those of Linnet with whom they associate in winter flocks. In courtship, flies up and down and displays red rump.

LESSER REDPOLL

TWITE

CROSSBILL—*LOXIA CURVIROSTRA.*[2]

Length 6½ ins. *Hen,* yellowish green. Cock sometimes yellow. Variable in colour and size. Bills of some birds cross left, others right. *Winter migrant*; local, chiefly in pine forests. Periodic invasions; also some residents. Scarce. *Nests* (Feb.-March) high in pine; 3-5 eggs, 1-2 broods. Cock helps feed, said not to build or incubate. *Food*: Caterpillars and larvæ. In winter, seeds, particularly conifer; cones prised open with beak. Young: regurgitated seeds. *Voice*: Both sexes have low, warbling song, early spring. Call, loud, shrill, "Gip Gip!" *Flight*: Circling. *Gait*: Hops; in trees, climbs with help of bill. *Manners*: Gregarious all the year. Flocks large in autumn. Roam about in winter.

NOTE.—The resident Scottish Crossbill (*L. c. scotica*) is said to have larger bill and longer wing.

SNOW BUNTING—*PLECTROPHENAX NIVALIS.*[2]

Length 7 ins. Plate shews winter plumage of cock. In summer, black and white, no colour. *Hen,* white dusky and colours browner. *Winter migrant* (Sept.-May) chiefly E. coasts. Fields and waste lands near sea. Some residents on high Scottish mountains. *Nests* (May-June) rock crevices; 5-7 eggs, 1 brood. Cock helps feed, does not build or incubate. *Food*: Gnats, etc.; later, seeds of grass and weeds. *Voice*: Song, low melodious warbling. Sweet, tinkling call notes. *Flight*: Hesitating, like butterfly. *Gait*: Runs, rarely hops. *Manners*: Gregarious in winter, feeding on the ground. In courtship, cock rises swiftly and circles down, singing, with tail and wings spread.

CROSSBILL

SNOW BUNTING

CORN BUNTING—*EMBERIZA CALANDRA.*[2]

Length 7 ins. *Sexes* alike. *Resident*, also winter migrant (in flocks). Local throughout United Kingdom. Hedges or trees in pasture, commons, downs. *Nests* (June) in hay, furze or low bushes; 3-6 eggs, 1-2 broods. Doubtful if cock helps at all. *Food:* Seeds of grasses and cereals, also beetles and insects. *Voice:* Song, Jan.-Aug., harsh, monotonous jingling as of broken glass, repeated for hours from bare branch or telegraph wire. *Flight:* Heavy and laboured, legs hanging down as if broken. *Gait:* Hops. *Manners:* Lethargic, sitting with drooped tail. In autumn, associates with Finches in stubbles.

YELLOW HAMMER—*EMBERIZA CITRINELLA.*[2]

Length 6¾ ins. *Hen* much duller, crown dull olive. After autumn moult, cocks browner. *Resident* throughout United Kingdom; also winter migrants. Commons and waste lands. *Nests* (Apr.-May) on or near ground in hedge-bottoms, gorse or banks; 3-6 eggs, 2-3 broods. Cock helps build, incubate and feed. *Food:* Seeds of cereals, grasses, weeds, insects, berries and fruit. Young: insects and macerated seeds. *Voice:* Song, mid-Feb. to end of Aug., "Little-bit-of-bread-and-no-cheese." Call, "Tritt!" *Flight:* Jerky, drooping, scattered. *Gait:* Hops. *Manners:* Inert, perches on bush-top or tree, whence he sings. Feeds on ground. In summer, searches lower trees for insects for the young.

CORN BUNTING

YELLOW HAMMER

CIRL BUNTING—*EMBERIZA CIRLUS.*[2]

Length 6 ins. *Hen* has no black or bright yellow, back spots larger. *Resident*, local, in S. England and Wales. *Nests* (May) like Yellow Hammer; 3-5 eggs, 2 broods. *Food*: Seeds of grasses, cereals, weeds. Young: insects. *Voice*: Song, much as Yellow Hammer, but lacking long final note. Call, " Tritt ! " *Flight*: As other Buntings. *Gait*: Hops. *Manners*: Shy, hides from view in tall trees. In autumn and winter, packs in stubbles.

REED BUNTING—*EMBERIZA SCHŒNICLUS.*[2]

Length 6 ins. After autumn moult, cock has black obscured by tawny fringes, upper surface feathers edged rufous, white of neck becomes sandy-brown. *Hen* is much browner. *Resident* throughout United Kingdom, except northern islands. Scarce in N. Scotland. Also summer and winter migrants. *Nests* (Apr.-May) on or near ground in marshy spots ; 4-6 eggs, 2-3 broods. Cock helps feed, said to help build and incubate. *Food*: Insects and larvæ, molluscs, crustaceans, seeds of cereals and grasses. Young: insects. *Voice*: Song (end Feb. to end July), slight, reedy, 4 or 5 notes, laboured. Call, " Tschee ! " *Flight*: Low, flitting, spasmodic, fluttering on alighting. *Gait*: Hops and walks. *Manners*: Frequents waterside, reeds, willows and alders. More sprightly than other Buntings. Feigns wounded if nest approached. Hen sits close.

CIRL BUNTING

REED BUNTING
(Cock and Hen)

STARLING—*STURNUS VULGARIS.*[2]

Length 8½ ins. *Sexes* alike. After autumn moult, each feather has buff or white tip which wears off by spring. *Resident,* also winter and summer migrants. General throughout United Kingdom. *Nests* (April) in buildings or any convenient hole, often ejecting Swifts and Woodpeckers; 5-7 eggs, 1-2 broods. Cock helps build, incubate and feed. *Food :* Insects, larvæ, worms, sometimes wheat, cherries, apples, berries, eggs and garbage. *Voice :* Song, all year (except July-Aug. moult) a series of very varied notes, wheezing, chuckling, whistling, clicks, coughs, kisses, mimicking all sounds. Alarm, "Krrrrr !" *Flight :* Alternately rapid vibration and sustained skimming. In packs, an orderly wheeling flight. *Gait :* Walks and runs ; rolling, bandy-legged. Hops when in a hurry or on rough surface. *Manners :* Very quarrelsome. Often sits on chimney-pots. In perching, droops wings. Feeds on sheep's backs. In worming, digs with open beak. Catches flies on wing and in water in autumn. Gregarious, except in breeding season, even then small packs of unmated birds. Autumn flocks associate with Rooks and Plovers. In winter, vast numbers roost, with evolutions and much noise, in colonies in reed beds, thickets and firs. In severe cold many go to coast.

NOTE.—The Shetland variety (*S. v. zetlandicus*) has a slightly longer wing and wider bill.

STARLING

GREEN WOODPECKER—*PICUS VIRIDIS VIRESCENS.*

Length 12 ins. *Hen* less crimson on head, moustaches black. *Resident* S. and E. England and Wales, in well-wooded country. *Bores* (mid-April) hole for nest, in hollow (usually soft-wooded) tree. Sometimes uses old hole ; 5-7 eggs, 1 brood. Cock helps bore, incubate and feed. *Food :* Ants, other insects, nuts and wild fruit. Young, said to get regurgitated food. *Voice :* Loud, laughing cry, shouts, January to late summer. Also other cries (4 syllable) threatening. Also, rarely, produces, by rattling beak against bough, a loud " drumming." *Flight :* Undulating, often alighting under a bough. *Gait :* On ground, body upright, awkward hops. On trees, runs, climbing with help of tail feathers. *Manners :* Has a strong pungent smell, energetic, watchful for enemies when boring, dodges behind trunk. Often after boring, ejected by Starling or Nuthatch. Pairs for life. Feeds mainly on ground. Long, barbed, protrusible, sticky tongue. Never perches, or climbs downwards. Sometimes takes two or three backward hops. Ascends spirally to top and then flies, dipping, to base of fresh tree, or, circling, returns to same.

GREEN WOODPECKER

SPOTTED WOODPECKER—*DRYOBATES MAJOR ANGLICUS.*

Length $9\frac{1}{2}$ ins. *Hen* smaller and has no crimson on head. *Resident* and fairly general in S. and mid-England and Wales, rarer up to S. Scotland. Oakwoods, hedgerows with large ashes, pollarded trees. *Bores* (May-June) in high rotten-cored trees, sometimes using hollow dead branches; 5-7 eggs, 1 brood. Cock bores (alone ?), helps incubate and feed. Returns to same tree yearly, but bores new hole. *Food:* Insects; later, fruit, ants, acorns, beechmast and fir seeds. Young: insects. *Voice:* No song. In spring, (and if excited), "drums" like Green Woodpecker. Alarm, "Chink!" A comparatively silent bird. *Flight, Gait and Manners:* Like Green Woodpecker, except that he is rarely on the ground, and frequents higher branches.

NOTE.—The Northern type, slightly larger (*D. m.²*) is a winter migrant in small numbers.

BARRED WOODPECKER—*DRYOBATES MINOR COMMINUTUS.*

Length $5\frac{1}{2}$ ins. *Hen* has white crown in lieu of crimson. *Resident* England and Wales, chiefly S. *Bores* (mid-May) in upper branches of high trees, or in old pollarded trees, usually choosing rotten wood; 4-6 eggs, 1 brood. Cock alone said to bore, helps incubate and feed. *Food:* Insects only. *Voice:* "Drumming" like Major. Repeated call (not when moulting), "Pick Pick Pick!" *Flight, Gait and Manners:* Generally like Major except that he descends more to ground for insects, still more prefers lofty trees and creeps along under side of branches. Very restless.

SPOTTED WOODPECKER

BARRED WOODPECKER

WRYNECK—*JYNX TORQUILLA.*[2]

Length 7 ins. *Sexes* alike. *Summer migrant*, chiefly
S. and E., April-Aug. Migrates singly. Gardens,
parks, woods. *Lays* (mid-May to June) in natural,
or old Woodpecker's, hole, to which it returns;
7-10 (even 14) eggs, 1 brood. Cock helps incubate and
feed. *Food:* Ants, all insects; later, small berries.
Young get boluses of insects. *Voice:* April to early
June; song, loud "Pee Pee Pee!" diminishing in
strength and pitch. Hen sits close and hisses. *Flight:*
Short, undulating. *Gait:* On ground, short jumps
with tail up; on tree, creeps, without using tail, and
perches. *Manners:* Skulking. Feeds, with sticky tongue
as Woodpecker, on trees and ground. Excited in courtship. Writhes neck when feeding. If seized, feigns death.

SWIFT—*MICROPUS APUS.*[2]

Length 7 in. *Sexes* alike. *Summer migrant*, April-
May to Aug., except extreme N., where passage.
Nests (May-June) in holes under eaves or in holes in
walls; 2-3 eggs, 1 brood. Cock helps build and
feed, does not incubate. Return yearly to nesting
sites. *Food:* Insects taken on wing (pellets).
Flight: Rapid and gliding, erratic, very high, almost
the swiftest of birds. *Gait:* Crawls, or perches, only
going to or from nest. *Voice:* Harsh, exulting
scream. *Manners:* Always on the wing. Suffer
from parasites. Fight (with claws) for nests with
Starlings and Sparrows. Cocks fly near nests,
squealing. Hens come out to feed in the evening.
When they retire, cocks rise high and are said to
sleep floating in air. Also roost in nests. Leave
without swarming as soon as young can fly.

WRYNECK

SWIFT

NIGHTJAR—*CAPRIMULGUS EUROPÆUS.*[2]

Length 10½ ins. *Hen* slightly smaller and without white spots on wing and tail. *Summer migrant*, May to early September, throughout United Kingdom. Local. Commons, moors, uncultivated ground. *Lays* (end May) on the bare ground; 2 eggs, 1-2 broods. Cock helps incubate and feed. *Food:* Beetles, moths, grasshoppers. Young: regurgitated insects. *Voice:* Churring sound as of tearing calico, except for a time in August, delivered from top bough of tree, or on ground, at night and morning. Rarer in day. In flight, "Co-ik;" alarm, "Quick Quick!" *Flight:* Swift, noiseless, circling. *Gait:* Runs or creeps, legs unseen. *Manners:* Sits on ground during day. Suffers much from parasites. Dust bather. Returns to same spot yearly. Cock arrives first. In courtship, wags tail like a dog and flies, smacking wings together above back. Feigns injury to decoy from eggs or young. Has favourite trees and perches lengthwise on bough. Hunts only after dark. Use of comb-claw unknown.

NIGHTJAR

KINGFISHER—*ALCEDO ATTHIS ISPIDA.*

Length 7½ ins. *Hen* has base of bill red. *Resident* in low-lying parts of England and Wales. Rarer in Scotland, especially north, very scarce in Ireland. *Burrows* a nest (end April) in steep banks of stream. Uses old nests ; 6-8 eggs, 1-2 broods. Cock helps bore (with bill, not claws) and feed. *Food :* Fish and fry, shrimps, rarely slugs, snails and leeches. Ejects pellets. *Voice :* Shrill note, musical " Tit Tit Tit ! " *Flight :* Low and very swift, sometimes hovering motionless. *Manners :* Sits still on favourite perch over smooth water into which it peers with head thrust forward. Plunges suddenly to seize fish and bears it back to the perch, against which he beats it. Swallows head first. Solitary, very pugnacious, shy, dashing off with repeated cry. Young are driven away as soon as they can feed themselves. Nests very dirty.

KINGFISHER

COLOUR GROUPING
OF THE SMALL BIRDS

Black—Blackbird (cock), Starling (spring), Swift.

Pied—Snow Bunting, Pied Flycatcher, Martin, Swallow, Water Wagtail, Barred and Spotted Woodpeckers.

Black-headed—Bullfinch, the Great, Coal, and Marsh Tits, and the cocks of Blackcap, Brambling (spring), Reed Bunting and Stonechat.

Brown—Blackbird (hen), Nightjar, Starling (winter), Swift, Wren and Wryneck.

Brown with Pale Breasts—Blackcap (hen), Greenfinch (hen), Sand Martin, Nightingale, Shrike, Sparrows, Stonechat (hen), Tree Creeper, the Garden, Reed, and Sedge Warblers, Whinchat and Whitethroats.

Brown with Spotted Breasts—Corn Bunting, Reed Bunting (hen), Fieldfare, Spotted Flycatcher, Larks, Linnet, Pipits, Redwing, Mistle Thrush, Thrush, Twite and Grasshopper Warbler.

White (the following, as well as Pied birds, shew white)—Reed Bunting (cock), Chaffinch, Dipper, Larks, Ring Ouzel, Tits, Wagtails and Wheatear.

Red—(the following shew red)—Bearded Tit, Goldfinch, Hawfinch, Kingfisher, Redbreast, Redstart, Redpoll, Woodpeckers, and the cocks of Chaffinch, Bullfinch, Crossbill and Linnet (spring).

Green—Chiffchaff, Crossbill (hen), Greenfinch (cock), Siskin, Blue and Great Tits, Yellow Wagtail, Willow and Wood Warblers, and Green Woodpecker.

Yellow (the following shew yellow)—Cirl Bunting, Goldcrest, Goldfinch, Greenfinch, Siskin, Yellow Hammer, Grey and Yellow Wagtails, Willow and Wood Warblers, and Green Woodpecker.

Blue—Kingfisher, Nuthatch and Blue Tit.

PART II

THE
LARGE BIRDS
(ALL THE REST)

DRAWN TO ONE-FIFTH NATURAL SIZE

THIS SPARROW IS DRAWN TO THE ONE-FIFTH
SCALE OF THE LARGE BIRDS FOR COMPARISON

RAVEN—*CORVUS CORAX.*[2]

Length 25 ins. *Female* smaller. *Resident* and winter migrant. Rare except in mountain districts. *Nests* (Feb.-Mar.) in cliffs, crags; 4-6 eggs, 1 brood. Male helps build, incubate and feed. Returns to same nest. *Food:* Omnivorous, mainly carrion. Sometimes kills wounded sheep, rodents, etc., Pellets. *Voice:* Deep, hoarse croak. Also a series of varied notes. Great mimic. Cork-popping. *Flight:* Bold, sweeping; flapping, slow start. In courtship, gambols in flight, closing wings and rolling round. *Gait:* Walks, seldom hops. *Manners:* Sagacious, crafty, mischievous, very hardy. Pairs for life. Combative when nest approached. Scolds or tears up turf in rage. Eats other birds' eggs and young. In remote places have been seen to roost noisily in great numbers. Flock in winter. Collect for Highland deer-stalking.

CHOUGH—*PYRRHOCORAX.*[3]

Length 16 ins. *Female* smaller and duller. *Resident* locally on west coasts. *Nests* (end April) cliff holes, caves, ruins; 3-5 eggs, 1 brood. Male helps build and feed, does not incubate. *Food:* Insects, crustaceans, worms, berries. In winter almost omnivorous. *Voice:* Ringing "Kchare." When excited, chattering note. *Flight:* Buoyant. *Gait:* Walks and runs rapidly. *Manners:* Vivacious, fond of hiding things; pairs for life; in courtship feeds female and rubs her head with beak. Solitary in nesting. Flocks in autumn. Aerial exercises.

RAVEN

CHOUGH

CARRION CROW—*CORVUS CORONE.*[2]

Length 20 ins. *Female* smaller and duller. *Resident* throughout Great Britain. Rare in N. Scotland; also winter migrants. *Nests* (April) in trees. In default, cliff ledges, bushes, or on ground; 4-5 eggs, 1 brood. Male helps build, incubate and feed. *Food :* Almost omnivorous, usually carrion. *Voice :* Harsh "Caar!" *Flight :* Steady, slow, heavy beating. *Gait :* Walks. *Manners :* Very cunning, not shy. Generally seen singly or in pairs. Seeks food from dawn to sunset. Cracks shell-fish and nuts by dropping them from a height. In courtship, fans tail and droops wings, and gambols in mid-air. Pairs for life. Breed in scattered pairs. Quarrelsome about building sites. Return to same spots and repair old nests. Roost in large flocks, also with Rooks and Jackdaws.

NOTE.—The stronger, bristled, beak and slower wing-beats most easily distinguish from Rook.

HOODED CROW—*CORVUS CORNIX.*[2]

Length 20 ins. *Female* smaller and duller. *Resident* in Ireland, Isle of Man and N. Scotland; also large winter migration (Sept.-April) to E. coast. *Voice :* As Raven. *Nests, Food, Flight, Gait and Manners :* As Carrion Crow. Perhaps more gregarious. Both are less exclusive than the Raven, mixing and inter-breeding with each other.

CARRION CROW

HOODED CROW

ROOK—*CORVUS FRUGILEGUS.*[2]

Length 19 ins. *Female* smaller and duller. Young not bald-faced. *Resident* and common throughout United Kingdom in tree-tops and fields. Also summer and winter migrants. *Nests* (Mar.-Apr.) in colonies in tree-tops; 3-6 eggs, 1 brood. Male helps build and incubate, and feeds female and young. *Food :* Chiefly worms, insects, slugs. In autumn, acorns, seeds, some grain. In winter almost omnivorous. *Voice :* 30-40 different notes, series of little gabblings punctuated by strident "Caw !" *Flight :* Steady, slow beating, but less slow than Crow. *Gait :* Walks, waddling; some sideway hops. *Manners :* Sedate, truculent. Gregarious. Out of breeding season feeds with Daws, etc., on fields and, leaving the rookery, roosts in trees in large flocks, very noisily. Playful antics in air with Daws and Plover. Rookery sometimes destroyed by one pair of Crows. Courting, feeds hen, fans tail.

JACKDAW–*CORVUS MONEDULA SPERMOLOGUS.*

Length 13 ins. *Female* has less grey. *Resident* throughout United Kingdom. Also summer and winter migrants. *Nests* (mid-April) in any hole, usually in buildings or trees; 4-6 eggs, 1 brood. Male helps incubate, build and feed. *Food :* As Rook, also eggs and young birds. *Voice :* High-pitched, querulous "A-aw !" Noisy. *Flight :* Rapid, wavering, with many games and tumblings in the air. *Gait :* Walks, swaggering. *Manners :* Pert, dapper, brisk. Thieves. Pair for life; devoted to mates and young. Gregarious with Rooks and Gulls in autumn and winter. Perches on sheep's backs. Courts like Rook; also raises crest and presses beak on breast to shew his hood.

ROOK

JACKDAW

MAGPIE—*PICA.*[3]

Length 18 ins. *Female* smaller. *Resident* throughout United Kingdom in wooded districts. *Nests* (April) high in trees; also hedges and bushes; 5-8 eggs, 1 brood. Male helps build, incubate (?) and feed. Inclined to build several nests. *Food :* Practically omnivorous—eggs and young birds. Young: insects, worms, mice and young birds. *Voice :* Chattering, with whistling notes in spring. *Flight :* Slow, wavering, with intervals of violent wing beats. Usually flies low. Balances with tail on alighting. *Gait :* Walks, hops sideways and runs. *Manners :* Jaunty, restless, inquisitive, wary, cunning. Feeds on ground. Flocks in winter and hoards food. Pairs for life. Nuptial gatherings in spring.

JAY—*GARRULUS GLANDARIUS RUFITERGUM.*

Length 14¼ ins. *Female* duller. *Resident* and common throughout Great Britain, except the Highlands. Local in Ireland. *Nests* (April-May) in fork of bush or tree; 4-6 eggs, 1 brood. Male helps build, incubate and feed. *Food :* As Magpie. *Voice :* A noisy screech; also low warblings mixed with imitations of animals and other birds. *Flight :* Freer than Magpie's. Balances on alighting with tail and claps wings open and shut. *Gait :* Walks and hops sideways. Hence "Jay-walking"? *Manners :* Alert, tireless, excitable, vociferous. Pairs for life. In the spring, sociable—at other times solitary. In winter hoards food.

NOTE.—The Irish variety (*G. g. hibernicus*) is darker and redder.

MAGPIE.

JAY.

CUCKOO—*CUCULUS CANORUS.*[2]

Length 12 ins. *Sexes* alike. *Summer migrant,* mid-April to early July (young leave in Sept.) throughout United Kingdom. Open woodland. *Lays* (May-June) or deposits with beak, single eggs in nests of other birds, frequently ejecting one or more of the owner's eggs. She uses, as foster parents for her young, almost all small birds, particularly Hedge Sparrow, Reed Warbler, Meadow Pipit and Pied Wagtail, and each Cuckoo has been said to keep mainly to one species; 2 clutches of 5-7 and 4-5 eggs. *Food:* Hairy caterpillars, insects, larvæ, spiders, occasionally seeds, grass, worm-eggs (pellets). Young get food of foster parents. *Voice:* Song "Cuckoo," mid-April to end of June, delivered bowing head and fanning tail. Hen has a bubbling sound. *Flight:* Low scouring, hawk-like. *Gait:* Hops clumsily. *Manners:* Returns yearly to defined districts, fiercely defended. Polyandrous. The young, when hatched, eject all other eggs and chicks from nest. Mobbed by small birds. Perch on tree-tops.

CUCKOO (Adult)

CUCKOO (Young)

BARN OWL—*TYTO ALBA.*[2]

Length 13 ins. *Sexes* alike. *Resident*, general throughout United Kingdom. Rare in Wales, Ireland and the Highlands. *Lays* (end April) in dark recesses in buildings, sometimes trees, rocks, etc. Uses same place year after year ; 4-6 eggs (sometimes even 11) ; 1-2 broods. Male helps feed, but does not incubate. *Food :* Almost entirely mice ; rarely rats, moles, squirrels, bats, rabbits, frogs, beetles and small birds. Pellets. *Voice :* Early part of year, weird shriek. " Screech Owl." Sometimes a loud snoring noise. When alarmed snaps jaws together making sharp noise. *Flight :* Silent and buoyant flitting ; short quick wing strokes ; seems to want ballast. *Manners :* Nocturnal, seldom hunts by day. Spends daylight hours standing upright and dozing on perch. Prefers human habitations. Stay-at-home bird. Eyes larger than any other bird's. Very soft plumage. Accumulates food in the nest which is used to live in. Said to bring back a mouse to the nest every fifteen minutes. *Gait :* Walks. Perches with two toes to the front, walks and stands on the level with three.

BARN OWL

LONG-EARED OWL—*ASIO OTUS*.[2]

Length 15 ins. *Sexes* alike; male sometimes paler. *Resident* throughout United Kingdom in pine-wooded districts; also winter migrants. *Lays* (March-April) in flattened tree nest of other birds or Squirrel drey. Sometimes on ground; 3-5 eggs, 1-2 broods. Male probably does not incubate, feeds hen and young. *Food:* Field mice, rats. *Voice:* Chirruping note when starting out at night. Female's nuptial call, long-drawn "Oo-oo-oo-oo!" Male has moaning note, smacking wings together. *Flight and Gait:* As Barn Owl. *Manners:* Nocturnal; mobbed by small birds; fierce when roused; spits like a cat. Avoids man. By day stands upright close to tree-trunk. Comparatively silent, in winter somewhat gregarious. Pellets.

SHORT-EARED OWL—*ASIO FLAMMEUS*.[2]

Length 14 ins. *Female* frequently darker. *Winter migrant* throughout United Kingdom (end Sept. to end Mar.); also passage and some residents, on moors and mountains. *Lays* (end April) in thick heather or hollow in grass; 4-8 eggs (up to 13), 1-3 broods. Male feeds but does not incubate. *Food:* Mainly voles, few mice. Pellets. *Voice:* Startled cry like a laugh; also hoots; hisses and clicks when angry. *Flight:* Free, twisting. *Gait:* Like Barn Owl. *Manners:* Feeds by night and day. Dwells on the ground in fens, meadows and commons. Nomadic in pursuit of food, follows vole plagues and small migrating birds. Noisy when young approached. Rises with loud "Quack!" Gregarious migrant.

LONG-EARED OWL

SHORT-EARED OWL

TAWNY OWL—*STRIX ALUCO SYLVATICA.*

Length 16 ins. *Female* larger. *Resident* and general in all wooded districts of Great Britain. *Lays* (mid-Mar.) in holes, usually in a tree, rarely in buildings; sometimes in nests of Crows, etc. In default of trees, occasionally on ground; 2-4 eggs, at times 6; 1 brood. Male does not incubate, but helps feed. *Food :* Like Barn Owl; more rats, fish. *Voice :* Call, " Too-whit, Too-whoo ! " Both sexes hoot. At dusk, call " E-wick." Calls most during breeding season. *Flight and Gait :* Like Barn Owl. *Manners :* Strictly nocturnal, solitary and jealous of any intrusion on his ground. Most noisy of all Owls. In courting, claps wings together over back (as does the Long-eared Owl). Spends the day in hollow tree-trunk or standing huddled against tree. Pellets.

LITTLE OWL—*CARINE NOCTUA MIRA.*

Length 8 ins. *Sexes* alike. *Resident*, recently imported and increasing. Found almost throughout United Kingdom. *Lays* (end April) in a hole in tree, wall, building or ground; 4-5 eggs, at times 7; 1 brood. Male does not incubate, but helps feed. *Food :* Voles, mice, birds and worms. *Voice :* Harsh " Cu-cu-cu ! " with exasperating monotony, both in spring and autumn. *Flight :* Like a Bat, erratic and often changing direction. *Manners :* Bold and savage, hunts by daylight as well as night. Vociferous in the breeding season. Shows great affection for its young. When excited, clicks beak and bows head.

TAWNY OWL

LITTLE OWL

HEN-HARRIER—*CIRCUS CYANEUS*.[2]

Length 19 ins. *Female* 21 ins. *Resident* (rare) in the Isles and Ireland; also winter migrants. *Nests* (end April) on ground in rough heather. Returns to same spot yearly; 4-6 eggs, 1 brood. Male does not incubate, but feeds female. *Food*: Birds, rats, mice, frogs, fish, insects and eggs. Young fed on nestling birds. *Voice*: Clear cry, " Ker-ker-ker ! " Usually silent. *Flight*: Buoyant, graceful, as Eagle's. Sometimes hovers. *Gait*: Walks. *Manners*: Quarters ground like Pointer in search of food, turning sharply with tail twist. Great rat-catcher, very strong, kills Black Cock with a single blow. In courtship, chase one another. In autumn, descend to lower lands.

MONTAGU'S HARRIER—*CIRCUS PYGARGUS*.

Length 18 ins. *Female* 19 ins. *Summer migrant* in small numbers to England, chiefly south. *Nests* (end May) on moorland in heather or gorse, or in growing corn; 4-6 eggs, 1 brood. Male does not incubate (?) but brings food. *Food*: Mice, small birds, reptiles, eggs, grasshoppers. *Voice*, *Flight*, *Gait and Manners*: Generally as Hen-Harrier. Very fond of eggs. Gregarious migrant.

HEN-HARRIER
(Male and Female)

MONTAGU'S HARRIER
(Male and Female)

GOLDEN EAGLE—*AQUILA CHRYSAËTUS*.[2]

Length 36 ins. *Female* slightly larger. The young have tail white above and barred dark brown across end. *Resident* in the Highlands. *Nests* (March-April) on tree or crag. Returns to old eyries in alternate years ; 2 eggs, 1 brood. Does not lay again if eggs are taken. Male does not incubate or feed, but brings food. *Food :* Grouse, ptarmigan, rabbits, hares, small mammals, birds and carrion. Also sickly lambs. Young fed, in turn, with livers, flesh, plucked and unplucked birds. *Voice :* Screams, a shrill squeal ending in abrupt bark. *Flight :* Slow, powerful, with much sailing and circling. *Gait :* Clumsy walk. *Manners :* Dignified, lethargic. Kills on the ground, seizing small victims by the head, large ones by head and haunch. Spreads wings to cover prey. Fond of bathing and basking in sun. Keeps nest clean for about 10 weeks, until 10 days before the young fly.

WHITE-TAILED EAGLE—*HALIÆËTUS ALBI-CILLA*.[2]

Length 28 ins. *Female* 34 ins. The young have pale feather edges, brown head and tail, and black beak. Now rare *Bird of Passage*, chiefly E. England, and chiefly young birds. Differs from Golden Eagle as follows :—*Food :* Water-fowl, hares, rabbits, rats, mice, carrion. Young fed on water-fowl, hares, rabbits and fish. *Voice :* Loud yelping, very shrill. *Flight, Gait and Manners :* Drops from great height when fishing and alights on sea. Sometimes fastens talons in too large a fish and is drowned. Males fight in the air with loud screams. At all ages this bird has more of shank unfeathered and more large scales on toes.

GOLDEN EAGLE

WHITE-TAILED EAGLE

BUZZARD—*BUTEO*.[3]

Length 20 ins. *Female* larger, 22 ins. *Resident* in Wales, the Lakes and Highlands and in the South West; also some winter migrants elsewhere. Rare. *Nests* (April) in cliffs and rocks, and sometimes trees; 2-3 eggs, 1 brood. Male helps incubate and feed. *Food:* Mice, rats, moles and young rabbits, reptiles, beetles, carrion and worms. *Voice:* A shrill, melancholy whistle, " Pee-yeou ! " *Flight:* Soar high in air in small parties. Slow, majestic, sailing in circles. *Gait:* Walks. *Manners:* Slow, phlegmatic, sluggish. Drops on its prey and kills it on the ground. Returns to same perch day after day and will sit there for hours. If female is killed, male will feed young alone.

KITE—*MILVUS*.[3]

Length 24 ins. *Female* slightly larger, duller, shorter tailed. *Resident* (a few pairs) in Wales. Occasional visitor to E. coast. *Nests* (mid-April) in trees; 2-3 eggs, 1 brood. Male does not incubate. *Food:* Offal, small mammals, birds, reptiles and fish. *Voice:* Long drawn, mewing cry, " Whew-heh-heh-heh ! " *Flight:* Majestic, soaring at great height. Hunts flying low, gliding. *Gait:* Walks. *Manners:* Remarkably graceful, powerful, cowardly, generally silent. Travels widely. Picks up rags and oddments for the nest.

BUZZARD

KITE

SPARROW-HAWK—*ACCIPITER NISUS.*[2]

Length 13 ins. *Female* 15 ins. *Resident* in all wooded districts; also winter migrants. *Nests* (April-May) on remains of Crow, Pie or Pigeon's nest against bole of tree; 4-6 eggs, 1 brood. Male helps to collect material, sometimes to incubate; feeds female and brings food for young. *Food:* Small mammals and birds, frogs. Young: small birds and mice. *Voice:* In spring, "Kick-kick-kick," uttered soaring high above nest. *Flight:* Low, beating hedges, only rising to clear them. Very swift and skilful in cover. *Gait:* Walks. *Manners:* Fierce and agile. Lurks at edges of woods and pursues victim till seized. Kills on the ground, under drooped wings, gripping with both feet. Plucks before eating. Keeps larder near nest.

PEREGRINE FALCON—*FALCO PEREGRINUS.*[2]

Length 15 ins. *Female* 19 ins. *Resident* on all coast cliffs and mountains. Also passage of young birds during winter. *Lays* (April) on cliff ledges; 2-4 eggs, 1 brood. Male (" Tiercel ") helps incubate and feed. *Food:* Mainly birds, also rabbits and rats. *Voice:* Powerful cry, " Hek-hek-hek ! " *Flight:* Very fast and agile. The rush when striking (" Stoop ") sounds like a rocket. *Gait:* Walks. *Manners:* Courageous, noisy. Returns to same spot year after year. Perches on crag, erect and still. Unerring hunter. Wheels round the eyrie uttering loud cries. If one bird is killed, survivor finds another mate.

SPARROW-HAWK
(Male and Female)

PEREGRINE FALCON
(Male and Female)

HOBBY—*FALCO SUBBUTEO.*[2]

Length 12 ins. *Female,* 14 ins. *Summer migrant* (May-Sept.) in England, mainly S.E. *Lays* (June) in old nest of Crow or Magpie; 2-4 eggs, 1 brood. Male does not feed young. *Food :* Mainly large insects; also small birds. *Voice :* Shrill clear cry, " Kee-kee-kee ! " *Flight :* The fastest known flier. Can strike down a Swift in flight. *Gait :* Walks. *Manners :* The Falcon of the woodlands. Seizes insects with the foot and transfers them to the bill in flight. Known to drop food into the nest so as to keep out of shot.

MERLIN—*FALCO COLUMBARIUS ÆSALON.*

Length 11 ins. *Female* 12 ins. *Resident* in Wales, Pennines, Scotland and Ireland. Winter migrant, over wider range. Wild moors and mountains. *Nests* (May) in scratched-out hollow, among heather or on cliffs; 4-5 eggs, 1 brood. Male helps incubate. *Food :* Small birds and large moths. *Flight :* Usually low, without the great " stoops " of Peregrine or Hobby. Does not often soar or glide. *Gait :* Walks. *Manners :* Very plucky. Sits on rocks and flies along streams or hedges. Pursues a victim, rising above it at the last to strike. In courtship, rises to a great height, calling, and then descends to the ground. If young threatened, protests with loud cries. Moves to lower ground in winter.

HOBBY
(Male and Female)

MERLIN
(Male and Female)

KESTREL—*FALCO TINNUNCULUS.*[2]

Length 14 ins. Very variable. *Female* shewn in plate. *Resident*, winter migrants and passage, throughout United Kingdom, tending south in winter. *Lays* (April-May) 4-6 eggs, 1 brood, on cliff ledges, in ruins, church towers, or other birds' nests. Male helps incubate. *Food :* Chiefly mice, also small birds, moles, reptiles and insects. Young fed by both parents on mice. *Voice :* Shrill clear cry, " Kee-kee-kee ! " Harsh chatter when assailed by small birds. *Flight :* Easy, steady ; hangs stationary in mid-air (" Wind-hover ") suspended by rapidly beating wings ; and sails. *Gait :* Walks. *Manners :* Travel singly or in small groups. Hunt by sight, dropping on to quarry. Silent if young threatened.

OSPREY—*PANDION HALIAETUS.*[2]

Length 22 ins. *Female* 24 ins. *Bird of Passage*, Sept.-May, chiefly young birds. Now practically extinct as resident. *Nests* (end April) in trees on islets in lochs. Male brings materials and helps incubate ; 2-3 eggs, 1 brood. *Food :* Fish. Both parents feed young. *Voice :* " Killy-killy-killy ! " When angry, loud shriek. When carrying food, " Fish-fish-fish ! " *Flight and Gait :* As Kestrel. *Manners :* Until approached, lethargic, then vicious. Plunges deep for prey. Sails round for hours holding fish in claws. Has outer toe reversible. Mobbed by small birds. Young hatched with open eyes.

KESTREL
(Male and Female)

OSPREY

CORMORANT—*PHALACROCORAX CARBO.*[2]

Length 36 ins. 14 tail feathers. Crest and white patches present only February to July. *Sexes* alike. *Resident* on all steep coasts. One colony 5 miles inland (Merionethshire). In winter, added migrants and southward movements. Abundant; often on inland waters. *Nests* (end April) on rocky ledge, rarely in tree, near water. Return to old nests; 3-5 eggs, 1-2 broods. Both sexes build, incubate and feed. *Food*: Fish, caught by short dives and usually killed on the surface. Young: partly digested food from parents' throat. *Voice*: Usually silent, harsh croaking when resting or alarmed. *Flight*: Rises laboriously, fast, powerful, regular rapid beats, outstretched neck and feet. Sometimes skims. Flies low except over land. *Gait*: Clumsy, swaying walk. Swims low, with beak uptilted, paddling alternate feet. If scared, shows neck only. Dives with jump into air. Under water, swims with feet only, striking simultaneously. *Manners*: Shy, wary, voracious, sociable, smelly and dirty at nest. Pellets. Breed harmoniously in colonies. Fish in roughest water. Rest on rock after feeding, erect with wings outspread. Can be tamed.

SHAG—*PHALACROCORAX ARISTOTELIS.*[2]

Length 28 ins. 12 tail feathers. Crest present only December to July. *Sexes* alike. *Resident* on rocky coasts, except from Isle of Wight to Northumberland. In winter, everywhere. Huge flocks on W. Rarer than Cormorant save in N. and W. Scotland. *Nests* (April) in sea caves and ledges; 2-5 eggs (usually 3); 2 broods. One bird builds, other carries the materials. Both incubate and feed. Differs from Cormorant as follows :—More purely marine, flies only over sea; pose less upright, neck curved, flight lower. Sex display with head and tail meeting, female stroking his neck with beak.

CORMORANT

SHAG

GANNET—*SULA BASSANA.*

Length 37 ins. *Sexes* alike. Birds in first year are dark brown flecked with white; the brown diminishes yearly until, after fourth or fifth moult, it has gone. *Resident* on Bass Rock, in Pembroke, W. Scotland and Ireland, in few large colonies. Migrate south, following herring, leaving from August-December and returning February-March, so that colonies are deserted only in January. *Nests* (April) on ledge of rock; 1 egg reared. Both sexes build, incubate (holding egg in foot) and feed. *Food:* Fish. Young: on semi-digested and, later, disgorged fish. *Voice:* Loud, harsh, strident cry. When leaving nest, a long wail. *Flight:* Easy and powerful skimming and sailing. *Gait:* Ungainly hops to edge of ledge. Masterly swimmer. *Manners:* Lives on the sea, gregarious only when nesting. Very quarrelsome. When fishing, circles at great height; on seeing prey, rises higher and plunges head first, obliquely, swallowing fish under water. Arrive at nests in pairs; probably mate for life. Courting displays, bowing, head-wagging and whetting beaks when they meet.

GANNET

GREY LAG-GOOSE—*ANSER.*[2]

Length 35 ins. *Goose* 30 ins. *Resident* in N. Scotland; also winter migrant and passage (Sept. to end April) to the coasts of United Kingdom, chiefly W. *Nests* (mid-April) in deep heather or marsh grass; 4-6 eggs, 1 brood. Gander does not help incubate, but guards goose and young. *Food:* Corn, grass, water plants. Young feed on water plants and insects, accompanied by both parents. *Voice:* Sonorous "Ackh Ackh!" *Flight:* Laboured, with measured wing-beats, powerful and rapid. Fly high in V or W formation. (" Skein " or " Gaggle.") *Gait:* Walks with ease and dignity. Swims lightly. *Manners:* Pairs for life, gregarious, keeps apart from other species. Essentially land birds. Feed by day unless frightened. At dusk retire to open space to sleep, often sea-shore. Young are led back to nest every night by goose and sleep under her wing. When alarmed, wander erratically, fatigue sometimes killing the young. In danger, gander flies away leaving family. Moult all flight feathers at once (July) and hide while unable to fly, but dive well. Very wary. Diminishing in numbers.

BEAN GOOSE—*ANSER FABALIS.*[2]

Length 34 ins. *Goose* 31 ins. *Winter migrant* (Oct.-April) chiefly on W. coasts. Ireland mainly in severe winters. *Nests* abroad. Note said to be slightly softer. Otherwise as Grey Lag.

GREY LAG-GOOSE

BEAN GOOSE

PINK-FOOTED GOOSE—*ANSER BRACHYR-HYNCHUS.*

Length 28 ins. *Sexes* alike. *Winter migrant* to Great Britain, chiefly to E. coasts, Sept.-Oct. to end April. *Nests* abroad. *Food :* Grain, autumn-sown wheat, aquatic plants. *Voice :* Hard metallic " Honk Honk ! " A long series of short, high notes if alarmed. *Flight, Gait and Manners :* As Grey Lag so far as known. " Gaggles " are of vast numbers. Call constantly as they fly. Increasing in numbers.

WHITE-FRONTED GOOSE—*ANSER ALBI-FRONS.*

Length 27 ins. *Goose* rather smaller. *Winter migrant*, Oct. to end April. Abundant in Ireland, local in England, chiefly in S.W. *Nests* abroad. *Food :* Young shoots of water plants, grass, clover, corn and wild fruits. *Voice :* Loud laughing cackle. " Laughing Goose." *Flight, Gait and Manners :* As Grey Lag so far as known. More of a marsh than corn-field species. The Grey Lag, Bean, Pink-Footed and White-Fronted are known as Grey Geese.

PINK-FOOTED GOOSE

WHITE-FRONTED GOOSE

BRENT GOOSE—*BRANTA BERNICLA.*[2]

Length 23 ins. *Sexes* alike. *Winter migrant* in great numbers to E. coast of England and Irish sea-coast. End Sept. to April. *Nests* abroad. *Food:* Sea-weeds, molluscs and crustacea. *Voice:* Loud, clanging, defiant, "Honk Honk, Torrick Torrick!" *Flight:* As Grey Lag. *Gait:* Walks gracefully, runs fast. *Manners:.* Gregarious, essentially a sea bird, never crosses high-water mark. Spends nights at sea, days on tidal flats in estuaries. Feed in line in close order, very wary. Sometimes when feeding at high tide, up-end like Ducks. At dusk the whole host flies out to sea together. Flies in V or W formation only for long journeys.

BARNACLE GOOSE—*BRANTA LEUCOPSIS.*

Length 25 ins. *Sexes* alike. *Winter migrant* to N.W. coasts of United Kingdom, Sept. to early May. *Nests* abroad. *Food:* Grass, aquatic reeds and insects, and crustacea. *Voice:* Coughing grunt, low and pleasing. *Flight:* Powerful, often very high. *Gait:* Can run swiftly. *Manners:* Markedly gregarious. Least wary of Geese. Less exclusively a sea goose than the Brent. Frequents rivers, inland, at high tide. Feeds by night on grass-covered islands and pastures near the sea. Very punctual as to dates of migration. Brent and Barnacle are known as Black Geese.

BRENT GOOSE

BARNACLE GOOSE

MUTE SWAN—*CYGNUS OLOR.*

Length 56 ins. *"Pen"* smaller and has smaller "berry" than "Cob." *Resident* throughout the U.K., semi-domesticated. Imported by Richard I. *Nests* (early April) on islet in lake or stream, close to water ; 5-12 eggs, 1 brood. Cob helps build, incubate and tend young. *Food :* Water plants and insects. *Voice :* Soft low notes when pairing. Pen, angry hissing when disturbed. Cob, defiant grunt when guarding nest. *Flight :* Deliberate, powerful, with loud creaking throb ; rises flogging water. *Gait :* Walks. *Manners :* Usually silent. Swims about with neck in "S" shape. Pairs for life, returns yearly to same nest. Pairing takes place on water. Cygnets will climb on back of Pen. Cob guards nest, "busking," swimming forwards with simultaneous foot-strokes, wings raised and head thrown back. Can kill a dog and will attack a man or boat-load of people. Up-end to feed. Moult all flight feathers together.

WHOOPER SWAN—*CYGNUS.*[2]

Length 60 ins. *"Pen"* smaller. *Winter migrant,* visiting irregularly the coasts of United Kingdom (Oct.-April). *Nests* abroad*. Differs from Mute Swan as follows :—*Voice :* Sonorous "Klung Klung l" in time with wing-beats. Sound of flight described as "whistling." "Whistling Swan." Noisier. Carries neck stiffly upright. Flocks fly in wedge formation. Small bodies in line.

* N.B.—Has nested in United Kingdom.

MUTE SWAN

WHOOPER SWAN

BEWICK'S SWAN—*CYGNUS BEWICKII.*[2]

Length 50 ins. *Sexes* alike. *Winter migrant*, mainly
N. and W. Commoner in severe winters. Differs
from Whooper only as follows :—Different beak and
note, more gregarious and more strictly maritime.

SHELDRAKE—*TADORNA.*[2]

Length 26 ins. *Duck* slightly smaller, duller and
lacking horn on beak. *Resident* on flat sandy coasts
of United Kingdom; also winter migrant. *Nests*
(April-May) in tunnel in sand, or rabbit-burrow,
sometimes ejecting rabbit; 7-12 eggs, 1 brood. Drake
does not incubate. *Food :* Small crustaceans, molluscs,
marine worms and seaweed. Young : the same,
helped by both parents. *Voice :* Noisy when feeding,
particularly Duck. Long drawn bark with few
quacks. Drake, with closed beak, makes a whistling
squeak ; clear trill when courting. *Flight :* Strong,
swift, with slow regular beats, like Goose. *Gait :*
Walks easily, swims lightly, high in water. Seldom
dives unless wounded. *Manners :* Monogamous,
gregarious, but flocks ("droppings") are small.
Frequent coasts, estuaries and some lochs. Beat
ground for worms, up-end. In courtship Drakes
raise necks and dip them suddenly, walking round the
Ducks. Short tussles. Both parents escort new-
born young to water, where several families combine
to form troops. Young are active, but slow to fly.
Duck lines nest with down.

BEWICK'S SWAN

SHELDRAKE

MALLARD (WILD DUCK)—*ANAS PLATYR-HYNCHA.*[2]

Length 24 ins. *Duck* shewn in plate, not to scale. Drake moults twice, May and September, losing power of flight and hiding during moult. Summer dress, resembling Duck, is called "Eclipse" dress. *Resident* throughout United Kingdom on fresh waters; also winter migrant and passage. *Nests* (April), 8-14 eggs, 1 brood, on ground in vegetation near water; rarely in hollow trees, old nests, etc., or away from water. *Food:* Minute organisms got by sifting water through beak, insects, worms, slugs, small frogs and fish, water plants, grain and acorns. Young feed on insects, accompanied by the Duck, and dive for food. *Voice:* Drake, low whistle courting, and loud "Quork!" Duck, alarmed, "Quark!" *Flight:* Straight, rapid, powerful, swishing. Light on water feet first. Spring clear of water when flushed. *Gait:* Walks. *Manners:* Monogamous, gregarious, often in huge flocks. Spend day afloat, flighting at dusk to feed, returning at dawn. Feed at night owing to persecution. Go to the coast in hard frost. Stamp in shallow water to stir worms. Up-end. Rarely dive. Pair on water. Duck leaves eggs only at dawn and dusk, and then covers them with down. She guards flappers from rain with wings; kills the sick. Drake guards the nest till moult, then leaves with other drakes. Parent stock of tame ducks.

MALLARD
(Drake and Duck)

GADWALL—*ANAS STREPERA*.

Length 21 ins. *Duck* in plate, not to scale. Drake, eclipse dress much as Duck. *Resident* E. Anglia and Scotland; also winter migrant, irregular. *Nests* (May) on dry ground near water, sometimes in woods; 8-13 eggs, 1 brood. Duck alone incubates. *Food :* As Mallard. *Voice :* Feeding, Duck chatters incessantly. Drake utters occasional deep croak. In courting, " Ep-ep-pair ! " *Flight :* Pointed wings give rapid flight. *Gait :* Walks ; swims high, tail up. *Manners :* As Mallard, markedly wary and timid, prefers reed-fringed lakes, usually near coast, migrates by night. Courtship calm.

WIDGEON—*MARECA PENELOPE*.

Length 18 ins. *Duck* in plate, not to scale. Drake, eclipse dress in summer. *Winter migrant*, throughout United Kingdom; also few residents in Scotland. *Nests* as Gadwall; 7-8, up to 10, eggs. *Food :* Almost wholly vegetable. *Flight :* In speed between Teal and Mallard, twisting. *Voice :* Most loquacious, pipes, closing wide open beak, " Whee-ou ! " Duck has contented purr and alarmed " Kraak ! " *Gait :* As Mallard. *Manners :* Shyest, wariest and most gregarious of ducks. Feeds on land and water, preferably salt. Prefers day feeding, but if harried feeds at night. Can sleep on rough sea. In court-ship, 5 or 6 drakes display to one duck, erecting necks, sitting up, flapping wings loudly. Sometimes fight.

GADWALL
(Drake and Duck)

WIDGEON
(Drake and Duck)

GARGANEY—*QUERQUEDULA.*[2]

Length 16 ins. *Duck* in plate, not to scale. Drake, eclipse dress June-Dec. *Summer migrant* to E. Anglia and Kent, Apl.-Aug. Rare passage S. and E. England. *Nests* (April) in hollow in ground, in meadow near water ; 7-11, up to 13, eggs ; 1 brood. Duck alone incubates. *Food :* Small fish, water insects, small molluscs and aquatic vegetation. Young : the same except vegetation, guided by Duck. *Voice :* A harsh " Quack ! " the courting Drake has a high-pitched rattle, " Cricket Teal." *Flight :* Active, unwieldy, powerful. Can rise almost vertically. Swoops at water and goes on. Swift and noiseless. *Gait :* Walks ; swims high. *Manners :* Frequents swamps and back-waters, up-ends, does not dive, feeds at night. Courting Drake swims round, spreading scapulars and ruffling head, then the pair follow each other, forcing water through beaks.

TEAL—*QUERQUEDULA CRECCA.*[2]

Length 14½ ins. *Duck* in plate, not to scale. Drake, eclipse dress mid-July-Oct. *Resident* throughout United Kingdom ; also summer and winter migrants and passage. *Nests* as Garganey ; 8-12, up to 16, eggs. *Food :* Water plants, insects, small molluscs. Young : insects, guided by both parents. *Voice :* Duck quacks low and hurried. Drake whistles. Young in packs in autumn, low chatter. *Flight :* Very swift and powerful, swerving ; rises almost vertically. " Spring." *Gait :* Walks. *Manners :* Frequent fresh water, except winter migrants on first arrival. Several drakes court one duck, monogamous. Drakes tend young, feigning injury. Duck will follow young even into captivity.

GARGANEY
(Drake and Duck)

TEAL
(Drake and Duck)

PINTAIL—*DAFILA ACUTA.*[2]

Length 28 ins. *Duck* in plate, not to scale. Drake, eclipse dress July-Oct. *Resident*, scarce and local in Scotland ; also regular winter migrant and passage, Sept. and mid-April, chiefly to S. and W. *Nests* (May) on dry ground under bush ; 7-10 eggs, 1 brood. Duck alone incubates. *Food :* Insects, molluscs, crustacea and water plants. Young : insects. *Voice :* Very silent. Drake gives low whistle in flight, musical " Quuck-quuck ! " in courtship. Alarm note, " Kraak ! " Duck at night, a low " Quack ! " *Flight :* As Mallard, but swifter. *Gait :* Walks ; swims high with tail up. *Manners :* Likes fresh water near sea. Very wary. Generally resembles Mallard. Goes to stubbles for grain in autumn, catches ephemerids on the wing. Drake helps Duck select nest. Associate with Widgeon.

SHOVELLER—*SPATULA CLYPEATA.*

Length 20 ins. *Duck* in plate, not to scale. Drake has eclipse dress. *Resident* throughout United Kingdom, local, chiefly N. and E. ; also winter migrant. *Nests* (April) on ground in rank vegetation ; 8-12 eggs, 1 brood. Duck alone incubates. *Food :* Mainly mud organisms obtained by " bibbling," grass and water plants. Young : water insects, guided by Duck. *Voice :* Drake, in flight, " Puck-puck ! " in courtship, low " Conk-conk ! " *Flight :* As Garganey, but making a rattling sound. *Gait :* Walks clumsily. *Manners :* Strictly fresh water bird, prefers bog and marshes. Feeds night and day. Catches ephemerids in flight. Courtship resembles Garganey. Sometimes polyandrous. Slow swimmer.

PINTAIL
(Drakes and Duck)

SHOVELLER
(Drake and Duck)

TUFTED DUCK—*NYROCA FULIGULA*.

Length 17 ins. *Duck* in plate, not to scale. Drake dons eclipse dress in May. *Resident* throughout United Kingdom (increasing); also winter migrant (Oct.-June) and passage. *Nests* (mid-May) in colonies near water among rushes, coarse grass or under bushes on islands or shore of lakes; 8-12 eggs, 1 brood. Duck alone incubates. *Food :* Water plants got by diving and eaten on surface, insects and small fishes. Young, guided by Duck, pick up food on surface or eat plants brought up by her. *Voice :* Flight and alarm note, loud grating " Currah ! " Courting notes (March), " Puck-puck ! " *Flight :* Strong. *Gait :* Clumsy walker ; quick, neat diver. *Manners :* Purely fresh water diver. Sociable with other diving ducks. Floats idly all day, swims or flies at evening to feeding grounds. Alarmed, sinks body and swims to open water. Slow to fly.

POCHARD—*NYROCA FERINA*.[2]

Length 19½ ins. *Duck* in plate, not to scale. Drake's eclipse dress, unlike duck, head and neck browner, breast dark pencilled grey. *Resident* in small numbers (increasing) mainly in N. and E., also winter migrant, very irregular in number and place. *Nests* (April-May) in mud and reed beds ; 6-11 eggs, 1 brood. Duck alone builds and incubates. *Food, Voice, Gait and Manners :* Generally as Tufted Duck, but courting note a low whistle. Go to salt water if icebound. On rising from water, splash along surface. Courtship calm, swimming round with extended neck.

TUFTED DUCK
(Drake and Duck)

POCHARD
(Drake and Duck)

SCAUP—*NYROCA MARILA.*[2]

Length 18 ins. *Duck* in plate, not to scale. Drake has eclipse dress. *Winter migrant* (mid-Sept. to mid-June) and passage, general round coasts of United Kingdom, few in S. Ireland. *Nests* abroad*. *Food:* Mussels, winkles, some seaweed. *Voice:* Discordant " Scaup ! " In courtship, note like Turtle Dove. *Flight:* Rises heavily, splashing, flies rapidly. *Gait and Manners:* Rarely in fresh water. Sociable. Parties of 12 or so for feeding. Congregate to rest on exposed banks in estuaries. A typical diving duck.

* N.B.—Has, lately, nested in extreme N.

GOLDENEYE—*GLAUCIONETTA CLANGULA.*[2]

Length 19 ins. *Duck* in plate, not to scale. Drake has eclipse dress. *Winter migrant* (end Sept. to mid-June), throughout United Kingdom, chiefly inland waters. *Nests* abroad, in a hollow tree. *Food:* Small crustacea, molluscs and small fish, some vegetable matter. *Voice:* Similar to Tufted Duck, harsh grunting expostulation. *Flight:* More ready to fly than other diving ducks and quicker in rising. *Flight:* Noisy. " Rattlewing " and " Whistler." *Gait:* Stands in an upright position, walks. *Manners:* Nervous, unsociable, commonest diving duck. Frequents both salt and fresh water. Swims with head well up. Seldom comes to land. Often five-sixths of time under water, as much as 23 seconds in one dive.

SCAUP
(Drake and Duck)

GOLDENEYE
(Drake and Duck)

LONG-TAILED DUCK—*CLANGULA HYEMALIS.*

Length 26 ins. with tail. *Duck* in plate, not to scale. Drake's eclipse dress only seen abroad. *Winter migrant*, Sept.-April, rare in S. and W. *Nests* abroad*. *Food :* Marine molluscs got by diving, crustacea, fish fry, seaweed. *Voice :* Call note of Drake, " Coal and Can'le Licht ! " *Flight :* Rises quickly from water. *Gait :* Walks ; swims high and enjoys rough sea. *Manners :* Maritime bird, feeding grounds well off shore. Lively and neat diver, flocks often dive simultaneously. More under than above water.

* N.B.—Has bred in United Kingdom.

EIDER—*SOMATERIA MOLLISSIMA.*[2]

Length 25 ins. *Duck* in plate, not to scale. Drake's eclipse dress is much blacker than in winter, with irregular markings on back. *Resident* in Northumberland, Scotland, and one place in Ireland ; also winter visitor in small numbers elsewhere. *Nests* (May) in large colonies on island coasts. Duck chooses site with Drake and builds alone ; 8-11 eggs, 1 brood. *Food :* Marine molluscs and crustacea. Young, tended by Duck, pick up food. *Voice :* Wailing note, sometimes heard in autumn, harsh grating call, very silent bird. *Flight :* Looks heavy, but is swift ; straight and low. *Gait :* Walks. *Manners :* Never inland, shy, dives in rough water, swallows small molluscs whole, chews up large ones. In courtship, Drakes rise in water and flap wings. Duck sits close and for a month never leaves nest. Valuable grey down.

LONG-TAILED DUCK
(Drakes and Duck)

EIDER
(Drake and Duck)

SCOTER—*MELANITTA NIGRA.*[2]

Length 20 ins. *Duck* sooty brown with whitish cheeks and throat. *Winter migrant* and passage (Sept.-June), throughout coasts of United Kingdom, chiefly E. England and N. Ireland ; also few residents in N. Scotland. Non-breeding birds remain whole year. *Nests* (June) in hollow in waterlogged moorland, among heather, or on islets ; 5-8 eggs, 1 brood. *Food :* Molluscs, marine plants, worms, small fish and insects. Young, guided by Duck, feed on small molluscs. *Voice :* Flighting call, harsh grating ; alarm, " Tuck-tuck ! " *Flight :* Swift, close to water, with whistling wings. *Gait :* Walks ; if disturbed, swims quickly, head forward and bobbing, with lateral leg strokes like Grebe. *Manners :* Gregarious, flocks of thousands. A heavy looking bird, rarely inland, never feeds near shore ; feeds by day in deep water. When feeding on an ebb-tide, the birds furthest out repeatedly rise and fly in over the heads of the others to form the last line. Swims with tail up, like Pintail, unless in haste.

VELVET SCOTER—*MELANITTA FUSCA.*[2]

Length 22 ins. *Duck*, dark brown, feathers edged grey, white wing-bar and whitish breast. *Winter migrant* and passage, mid-Sept. and May, chiefly to E. coast of United Kingdom. *Nests* abroad. *Food :* Almost exclusively marine molluscs. *Voice, Flight, Gait and Manners :* As Scoter.

SCOTER

VELVET SCOTER

GOOSANDER—*MERGUS MERGANSER.*[2]

Length 26 ins. "Sawbill." Eclipse dress like Duck except for black ring round neck. *Duck*, 24 ins., shewn in plate, not to scale. *Resident* in N. Scotland on fresh waters. Rapidly increasing. Winter migrant (comes late Sept.) to parts of English coast. *Nests* (April) in holes in trees or banks, by river-sides, returning to old nests ; 7-12 eggs, 1 brood. Drake deserts when Duck begins to sit. *Food :* Fish, chiefly trout, caught by diving, some insects and plants while breeding. *Voice :* Harsh gutteral " Quack ! " ; call, low whistle heard early spring and late autumn. *Flight :* Straight and swift, usually down centre of stream. Rises pattering along water. *Gait :* Sits and walks upright and fairly fast. Will shuffle on breast to water. Swims very swiftly, half submerged. If scared, shows only head. Dives by sinking and swims swiftly under water, probably with feet alone. *Manners :* Very voracious, shy and wary, chiefly fresh water bird. Fish often brought to surface for eating, then bird stretches its neck and drinks. Displays in November, stretching neck, gulping, raising chest with beak down, kicking water backwards. Pairs go to breeding grounds March and April.

GOOSANDER
(Drakes and Duck)

MERGANSER—*MERGUS SERRATOR.*

Length 24 ins. "Sawbill." Eclipse dress like Duck, except shorter crest, flanks slate-grey. *Duck*, slightly smaller, shewn in plate, not to scale. *Resident* in N. and W. Scotland and Ireland, inland waters and coasts. Winter migrant (comes late Sept.) and passage (Oct. and May) on English coasts. *Nests* (May-June) in hollow in ground, shelter in rocks on island, by fresh or salt water. Well-trodden track to nest; 6-9 eggs, up to 16; 1 brood reared. Drake does not help, but stays about. Back to old nests. *Food*: Small fish, molluscs, crustacea (caught by diving), some insects, worms and plants while breeding. *Voice*: Usually silent, rough purring double note in courtship. Duck quacks when disturbed. *Flight, Gait and Manners*: Generally as Goosander. Sometimes up-ends. Mostly found in estuaries. Young collected into packs under one Duck. Gregarious in winter. Pair in March.

SMEW—*MERGELLUS ALBELLUS.*

Length 17½ ins. "Sawbill." Eclipse dress like Duck, but retains dark bands on fore-breast. *Duck*, 16 ins., shewn in plate, not to scale. *Winter migrants* (chiefly immature) to coasts and inland waters, mainly E. coast, Sept.-May. *Nests* abroad. *Food and Voice*: As Goosander. *Flight*: Swift and rapid. Takes to water feet first, rises pattering along. *Gait*: Swims high with arched neck; if alarmed, sinks body. Said to swim with wings under water. *Manners*: Seen with Goosanders and Goldeneyes whom it can outstrip in flight.

MERGANSER
(Drakes and Duck)

SMEW
(Drake and Duck)

HERON—*ARDEA CINEREA.*[2]

Length 37 ins. Comb on middle toe. *Sexes* alike.
Resident throughout United Kingdom. *Nests* (Feb.)
in "heronries" of great age, in tall tree-tops;
3-5 eggs, 1-2 broods. *Food :* Fish, frogs, beetles,
young water birds, mice, rats, voles. *Voice :* Harsh,
powerful "Frank!" often uttered on the wing.
Flight : Swift, slow-beating, with head recurved and
legs stretched out. *Gait :* Slow, stalking walk.
Wades deep and can swim for a short way. *Manners :*
Stands with head sunk on shoulders or, when feeding,
stands or wades slowly, peering forwards into water.
Spears prey with bill. Large fish taken to land.
Displays, strutting and wing-flapping. Birds gather
at heronries in January. Oils feathers with beak
from patches of "powder-down."

NOTE.—A census taken for "British Birds" in 1928 found
3,800 breeding pairs, in 256 sites, in England and Wales.

BITTERN—*BOTAURUS STELLARIS.*[2]

Length 28 ins. Comb on middle toe, frill erectile.
Sexes alike. *Resident,* very few, Norfolk. Lately
re-established. Elsewhere irregular visitor to most
marshy spots. *Nests* (Mar.-May) in reed beds;
3-6 eggs. Both parents feed young on regurgitated
food. *Food and Flight :* As Heron. *Voice :* Harsh
scream, flying. Male "Booms" (head up and bill
closed) like a bellowing bull, Jan.-June. *Gait :*
Walks or runs, head low, shoulders high. *Manners :*
Nocturnal; passes day in thick reeds. When
alarmed, "freezes" with bill and neck vertical.
Sometimes crouches with head drawn in, then
thrusts up fiercely. "Booming" male answers male.

HERON

BITTERN

STONE CURLEW—*ŒDICNEMUS.*[3]

Length 16 ins. *Sexes* alike. *Summer migrant*, end March-Oct., on bare stony soil and commons of S. and E. counties ; also a few residents in Cornwall. *Nests* (April-May) in hollows in open spaces ; 2 eggs, 1 brood reared. Male helps incubate and guide young to feed. *Food :* Insects, also small mammals. *Voice :* Rare calls by day ; at night, long wailing " Cour-li-vee ! " *Flight :* Low, clears nearest obstacle, then glides to earth. *Gait :* In approaching or leaving nest, head low and short, paddling paces, using cover. *Manners :* Silent, stealthy, very wary. In courtship, silent and dignified posturing. Mate of sitting bird stands guard. Male scrapes dummy nests. When nest approached, both parents slip away on foot, young lie flat with neck out. Pack in autumn. Become nocturnal. Wild fluttering dances and flights to marshes for food. Return to nesting ground at dawn.

RED-NECKED PHALAROPE—*PHALAROPUS LOBATUS.*

Length 7½ ins. *Female* larger and brighter. Winter plumage, grey and white. *Summer migrant*, very rare (May-Aug.), to the Isles ; also rare visitor to E. coasts. *Nests* (May-June) on tussock of grass in marsh ; 4 eggs, 1 brood reared. Male helps build and takes chief part in incubation and care of young. *Food :* Insects, worms, small fresh water and marine life. Young : insects. *Voice :* Low " Pleep-pleep ! " *Flight :* Graceful and rapid. *Gait :* Runs and walks. Swims buoyantly with head set back. *Manners :* Tame, jerky, energetic. Usually swims far out at sea. Female does most of courting and keeps guard while male is on nest.

STONE CURLEW

RED-NECKED PHALAROPE

WOODCOCK—*SCOLOPAX RUSTICOLA.*[2]

Length 14½ ins. *Sexes* alike. *Resident*, winter migrant (Oct.-Nov. to March) and passage. In wooded districts throughout United Kingdom; local. *Nests* (March) in depression among dead leaves; 4 eggs, 1-2 broods. Female alone incubates. Male helps feed. *Food:* Mainly worms, got by listening, stamping and probing; also slugs, insects, crustacea and molluscs. *Voice:* In courtship, deep repeated croak, varied by shrill screech. *Flight:* Rises silently, darts rapidly hither and thither through foliage, straight and swift across country. *Gait:* Walks. *Manners:* Shy, sleeps among low trees by day. Solitary. Sits close. Very acute hearing. Feeds by night in springs, marshes and muddy ditches. Cock's nuptial display (" Roding "), slow flight, half-hour morning and evening, plumage fluffed out and uttering call. Female carries young away from danger; feigns injury. Leave and enter woods by same glade. Migrate at night in great numbers, females arriving first. Many perish at lighthouses. In frost, move to the coasts. In severe winters drift to S.W. Ireland.

GREAT SNIPE—*CAPELLA MEDIA.*

Length 11 ins. *Sexes* alike. 16 tail feathers. *Bird of passage*, usually young birds, Aug.-Oct., rarely returning in spring. Principally S. and E. England. *Nests* abroad. *Food:* As Woodcock. *Voice:* Has several notes, but rises silently. *Flight:* Slow on wing, without zigzags, flies heavily. *Gait and Manners:* While in United Kingdom, similar to Snipe, except that it is a solitary bird and frequents drier sites.

WOODCOCK

GREAT SNIPE

SNIPE—*CAPELLA GALLINAGO.*[2]

Length 10½ ins. *Sexes* alike. 14 tail feathers. *Resident*, winter migrant (Oct.-Nov. to March) and passage. On moors and marshes throughout United Kingdom, rarer southwards. *Nests* (April) in long moor grass or rushes; 4 eggs, sometimes 2 broods. Male does not incubate, but both parents feed for first few days and then lead young to feeding ground. *Food :* As Woodcock. *Voice :* Deliberate " Chipper ! "; when flushed, " Scape ! " *Flight :* Very swift, corkscrew zigzag for 50 yards, then straight away to a distance. *Gait :* Strutting walk, with flirting tail and drooped wings. *Manners :* Lethargic habits, ravenous appetite. Spends day on moor and marsh, and " flights " at evening to ditches and bogs. Both sexes display in March, flying high and " drumming " with tail feathers in descent. " Heather Bleater." Dread frost and move to coasts. In severe winters drift to S.W. Ireland. Snipe are often in small parties or " Wisps."

JACK SNIPE—*LYMNOCRYPTES MINIMUS.*

Length 7½ ins. *Sexes* alike. 12 tail feathers. *Winter migrant* (Sept.-April) and passage, throughout United Kingdom. *Nests* abroad. Differs from the Common Snipe as follows :—Rarer ; less dependant upon animal food ; slower on the wing, with less marked turns and twists and much shorter flights, holding bill downwards ; solitary bird ; sits even closer ; often rises silently. Call, when uttered, less loud. Suffers less from frost.

SNIPE

JACK SNIPE

KNOT—*CALIDRIS CANUTUS.*[2]

Length 10 ins. *Sexes* alike. Marked seasonal change. *Bird of passage* and winter migrant (Aug.-May). *Nests* abroad. *Food:* Insects, worms, crustacea and molluscs; also vegetable matter. Young: insects and larvæ. *Flight:* Strong, capable of sustained flight. *Gait:* At rest, stands on one leg and will hop off without using the other. Walks and wades breast high. *Voice:* Clear grunting note, "Knut Knut!" used in flight. *Manners:* Generally as Dunlin. Packs closer than any other wader. Day and night feeder. Young arrive first.

SANDERLING—*CROCETHIA ALBA.*

Length 8 ins. *Sexes* alike. Marked seasonal change. *Bird of passage* and few winter migrants (Aug.-May). Some non-breeders spend summer. *Nests* abroad. *Food:* As Knot. *Voice:* Sharp "Quick Quick!" in flight; on beach, rapid "Wee Whit!" *Flight:* Quick, with quivering wings. *Gait:* Very rapid run with wings uplifted. *Manners:* Very silent, unless disturbed. Young and old birds come together. Associate with Dunlins and Ringed Plover on sea-shore. Also visit margins of inland waters. Prefers sand to mud, commoner on beach than estuary. Small flocks when feeding.

KNOT
(Summer and Winter)

SANDERLING
(Summer and Winter)

DUNLIN—*EROLIA ALPINA SCHINZII.*

Length 7½ ins. *Sexes* alike. Marked seasonal change. *Resident*, winter and summer migrant and passage. Breeds on high moors, sometimes marshes, chiefly from Pennines northwards; when not breeding, found on all our coasts. *Nests* (May) on ground in grass or heather; 4 eggs, 1 brood reared. Male helps incubate and watches. Both tend young. *Food:* As Knot, but no vegetable. *Voice:* Call, a clear whistle, "Trui!" Alarm and flight call, a long "Purre!" Chatters while feeding. *Flight:* Swift, swerving and rolling. Spring flight, soaring high and floating down with trilling song. *Gait:* Mincing; runs swiftly; swims across pools. *Manners:* Sedate, very jealous. Commonest of all shore birds. Associates with other waders. In courtship, male flies up to female and raises one wing. False nests. Feigns injury. Taps and probes for worms on mud flats in large flocks. When disturbed, wheel out to sea and back. Stand head to wind, bobbing, when feeding. Sleep at high water. Flocks appear cloud-like owing to simultaneous evolutions. Gregarious night traveller.

NOTE.—The Lapland type (*E. a.²*), seen in winter and passage, is said to be browner in summer than our resident.

LITTLE STINT—*EROLIA MINUTA.*

Length 6 ins. *Sexes* alike. In winter, rufous colouring replaced by ash-grey. *Bird of passage* in small numbers. Commonest in E. England Aug.-Sept., rarely returning May-June. *Nests* abroad. Differs from Dunlin as follows:—Also eats seeds. Voice softer, triple call, "Tchik Tchik Tchik!" Frequents sewage farms. Does not probe for worms.

DUNLIN
(Summer and Winter)

LITTLE STINT

COMMON SANDPIPER—*TRINGA HYPOLEUCOS.*

Length 8 ins. *Sexes* alike. In winter, upper parts more uniform. *Summer migrant*, April-Sept., rarely S. and E.; also passage. Very rare residents. *Nests* (end May) in grass, or on shingle, near rapid stream; 4 eggs, 1 brood reared. *Food:* Insects, larvæ, worms, fresh water shrimps and crustacea. *Voice:* Clear musical note repeated three times, "Wheet!" Male has trilling song in spring while soaring and descending on quivering wings. *Flight:* Low, frequently crossing the river, on long pointed wings, quick beating and skimming. *Gait:* Runs nimbly, swims easily, dives if in danger. *Manners:* Lively, restless and loquacious. Solitary. When standing, bobs head and jerks tail. Holds up wings when alighting. Perches in bushes. Comes down to estuaries in July.

GREEN SANDPIPER—*TRINGA OCHROPUS.*

Length 9½ ins. *Sexes* alike. Under-wing, black. In winter, upper parts uniform olive-green. *Bird of Passage* throughout United Kingdom (April-May and August onwards). Sometimes winters chiefly in E. and S. *Nests* abroad. *Food and Voice:* As Common Sandpiper. *Flight:* Rises silently, but pipes in flying. Towers high, turning and twisting. *Gait:* As Common Sandpiper. *Manners:* Very shy and wary. An inland species. Frequents streams and marshes in wooded country. Solitary. Flocks only on migration. Remains in same place for weeks. Perches on branches, posts and rails. Has a strong smell.

> NOTE.—The Wood Sandpiper (*T. glareola*) has pale grey under-wing and slightly longer legs. It is an autumn bird of passage to E. coasts of England, uncommon in spring; less shy and rarer. Has bred in U.K.

COMMON SANDPIPER

GREEN SANDPIPER

CURLEW-SANDPIPER—*EROLIA TESTACEA.*

Length 8 ins. *Sexes* alike. Marked seasonal change. *Bird of passage,* chiefly to E. and S. coasts, Aug.-Sept. (Ireland, Dec.), returning mid-March to June. *Nests* abroad. Differs from Dunlin as follows : *Voice :* Call on rising, "Twee Twee Twee"; also has a whistling note. *Flight :* More undulating and less erratic. Frequents inland localities as well as coast.

PURPLE SANDPIPER—*EROLIA MARITIMA.*[2]

Length 8 ins. *Sexes* alike. Marked seasonal change. *Winter migrants,* young in Aug., adults Oct., leaving April-May. *Nests* abroad. Differs from Dunlin as follows :—Also eats seeds. *Voice :* Rather silent ; note, a piping "Wheet !" *Flight :* More direct than most Sandpipers. Will swim on calm sea. Very tame. Frequent rocky coasts rather than mud flats, feeding at ebb-tide among seaweed.

CURLEW-SANDPIPER
(Summer and Winter)

PURPLE SANDPIPER
(Summer and Winter)

RUFF & REEVE—*PHILOMACHUS PUGNAX.*

Length 12½ ins. Plate shews Ruff in winter plumage.
Reeve, 10 ins., similar. Ruff grows nuptial plumes
(as inset) for 6 weeks (May-June), the colours of
which vary with each individual. *Bird of passage*,
Aug.-Sept. and April, along E. coast. Extinct as
resident. *Food :* Insects and worms. *Voice :* Loud,
shrill whistle. *Gait :* Walks erect without jerking
head. *Manners :* Mainly young birds visit us.
Found on coast, inland waters and sewage farms.
Very silent. Probes mud, but not deeply. Feeds
by night and day. Migrates at night. Promiscuous ;
elaborate crouching, sexual display or " lek."

BAR-TAILED GODWIT—*LIMOSA LAPPONICA.*[2]

Length 14-18 ins. *Sexes* alike. Female larger. Marked
seasonal change. *Bird of passage*, April-May and
Aug.-Oct.; also sometimes winter, and rarely summer,
migrants. Chiefly to E. and S. coasts in very varying
numbers. Extinct as resident. *Food :* Marine
invertebrates. *Voice :* Harsh, barking flight-call,
" Kew-it ! " While feeding, a wheezy chattering.
Flight : Swift, strong wing-beats, neck bent up. Rises
heavily. Twisting and side-slipping. *Gait :* Deliberate
walker and deep wader. Will sidle along after tide on
one leg. *Manners :* Rests with Knots, Oyster Catchers,
etc., at high tide. Feeds on the water side of
shorter-legged birds. In feeding, bores or works bill
horizontally. Young, very tame on arrival.

RUFF
(Winter and Spring)

BAR-TAILED GODWIT
(Summer and Winter)

CURLEW—*NUMENIUS ARQUATA.*[2]

Length 23 ins. *Sexes* alike. In winter, paler.
Resident and winter migrant (Aug.-Nov.). Breeds
on moors and highlands throughout United Kingdom
(Mar.-Apr. to July-Aug.), at other times is on coasts.
Nests (April) in rushes or depression in ground;
3-5 eggs, 1 brood reared. Male helps incubate and
tend young, and guards nest. *Food :* Insects, worms,
crustacea, molluscs and berries. Swallows sand and
grit. *Voice :* Wild, far-reaching " Cur-lew ! "; also
long bubbling note. *Flight :* Rises heavily. Swift,
with slow-measured beat, with skimming intervals,
legs stuck out behind. Flocks fly in V form. *Gait :*
Walks and wades ; swims easily. *Manners :* Most
wary of all birds. Noisy, gregarious. Warns other
birds of danger. Feeds day and night on sand flats
and rocks. Goes inland at high tide and waits for
ebb, of which it knows the moment. Courtship dance
as Redshank. False nests. Feigns injury with eggs,
not chicks. Bold in defence of nest. Sometimes
perches on trees and rails. Migrates in huge numbers.

WHIMBREL—*NUMENIUS PHÆOPUS.*[2]

Length 17 ins. *Female* 19 ins. *Bird of passage*, April-
May, returning July-Sept., throughout United Kingdom ; also a few summer migrants to the Isles.
Nests abroad. Differs from Curlew as follows :
Shriller voice. " Titterel." More rapid flight.
Much less shy. Not exclusively sand-flat feeder,
frequenting pasture lands and saltings. Scatter in
twos and threes when feeding, and call to each other
all night.

CURLEW

WHIMBREL

REDSHANK—*TRINGA TOTANUS.*[2]

Length 12 ins. *Sexes* alike. In winter, general colour more ashy. *Resident*, summer and winter migrants. Found all the year on coast, breeds throughout United Kingdom in low-lying meadows near rivers. Rarer in Wales, S. Ireland and the Isles. *Nests* (April) in tussocks, sometimes on high moorland; 4 eggs, 1 brood reared. Male helps incubate and guards. *Food :* As Dunlin; also berries. *Voice :* Clear, melancholy call, "Too-oo-ee!" *Flight :* Swift and noisy; close formation, changing front, not wheeling. *Gait :* Walks; can wade, swim and dive. *Manners :* Noisy, restless, vigilant. Increasing. Scattered in small groups or pairs. Fond of perching. Bob heads and sway bodies when feeding. In courtship, male raises wings, then half lowers and trembles them rapidly, marking time. Also hovering flight with bubbling song. Sit close. Bold if nest approached, attack dogs. Sometimes follow plough.

GREENSHANK—*TRINGA NEBULARIA.*

Length 13 ins. *Sexes* alike. In winter, upper parts greyer and under parts whiter. *Summer migrant* (rare), to Highlands and Isles; elsewhere passage. Found on coastal marshes and lakes. *Nests* in heather (May) near a loch in shelter of a rock; 4 eggs, 1 brood reared. Male, alone (?), incubates. *Food :* As Dunlin, also frogs and fry. Differs from Redshank as follows :—Louder voice, but less garrulous; less sociable. Seldom bores, preferring shrimps and small fish.

REDSHANK

GREENSHANK

GOLDEN PLOVER—*PLUVIALIS APRICARIA.*[2]

Length 11 ins. *Female* less black on breast. Marked seasonal change. *Resident* on moors and mountains throughout United Kingdom, chiefly N.; also winter migrant. *Nests* (April-May) *or lays* in scraped hollow on bare ground or heather; 4 eggs, 1 brood reared. *Food :* Worms, slugs, snails, insects, seeds, molluscs, crustacea. Swallows grit. Young: insects, guided by both parents. *Voice :* Clear, wild, far-reaching call-note, " Tlu-ee ! " Love song, double note like trill. Alarm, " Kop ! " *Flight :* Quick wing strokes and rapid wheeling. Nuptial flights. *Gait :* Runs lightly, often with uplifted wings. *Manners :* Gregarious, shy. Moves to hills in March. After breeding season pack and go to lowlands and coast. Frequent arable and pasture. When feeding, alternate runs and stops. Run sideways or backward to keep an eye on intruders. Migrate by night in V formation.

> NOTE.—The more northern form has been separated (as *P. a. altifrons*). It is distinguished in summer by a wider white line over the eye and slightly yellower colouring.

GREY PLOVER—*SQUATAROLA.*[3]

Length 11 ins. *Sexes* alike. Marked seasonal change. *Passage* (Sept.-Nov. and May), also a few winter migrants. *Nests* abroad in far N. *Food :* Small marine life. *Voice :* Courting song, a treble whistle ; call-note, a double whistle ; alarm, a single whistle. Similar to Golden Plover, but shriller. *Flight, Gait and Manners :* Generally as Golden Plover. Slower and more powerful flight. Larger, bolder and rarer. Keeps more to coast. Migrates both by day and night. Fly about late at night, calling.

GOLDEN PLOVER
(Summer and Winter)

GREY PLOVER
Summer and Winter

RINGED PLOVER—*CHARADRIUS HIATICULA.*[2]

Length 7¾ ins. *Female* has less well-defined black collar. *Resident* on coasts throughout United Kingdom and many places inland; also winter migrant (gregarious) and passage. *Lays* (May) 4 eggs in slight depression in fine shingle or broken shells. Often nests inland. Probably 2 broods. Eggs often left in sun. Male helps incubate. *Food :* Small marine life, insects. Young feed, guided by both parents. *Voice :* Wild and sorrowful, " Tulip ! " *Flight :* Very graceful and rapid. Often fly in pairs. *Gait :* Runs with short steps, often holds wings straight up for several seconds when standing. *Manners :* One of the commonest shore birds. Agile, lively, sociable. Associate with Dunlins and other waders. When disturbed, they circle out to sea and back. If nest approached, feign injury. In autumn, unite in flocks.

KENTISH PLOVER—*CHARADRIUS ALEXAN-DRINUS.*[2]

Length 6¾ ins. *Female* duller, with no black on crown and brown for black on neck. In winter there is no black nor rufous in the plumage. *Summer migrant* (April-Sept.) and passage. Sussex and Kent, and rarely up E. coast to Yorks. Differs from Ringed Plover as follows :—*Lays* 3 eggs, only 1 brood. *Voice :* Shriller and more flute-like.

RINGED PLOVER

KENTISH PLOVER

DOTTEREL—*EUDROMIAS MORINELLUS.*

Length 9 ins. *Sexes* alike. In winter, black and red on under parts become white. *Summer migrant* (May-Sept.) to Lakes and Scotland; also passage. *Lays* (May-June) in slight mossy depression on summits usually above 2,000 ft.; 3 eggs, 1 brood reared. Male helps incubate. *Food :* Insects, worms and molluscs. *Voice :* Low plaintive whistle. Harsh alarm note and soft twitter. *Flight, Gait and Manners :* Generally as Ringed Plover. Less shy and active than other Plovers. Rarely at seashore. Stretches out wing and leg before moving. Travel from S.E. coast to breeding haunts in "trips" of 5 to 20. Sociable breeders. Diminishing.

LAPWING—*VANELLUS.*[2]

Length 12 ins. In winter, no black on throat. *Female* has shorter crest and more pointed wing. *Resident* and general throughout United Kingdom; also summer and winter migrants and passage. *Nests* (Mar.-Apl.) on open ground; 4 eggs, 1 brood reared. *Food :* As Golden Plover. *Voice :* Courting, "Willuch Willuch !" and "Coo-whee !" Alarm, "Pee-wit !" *Flight :* Heavy flopping. Alternations of wild zigzag frenzy. *Gait :* Walks; runs rapidly with long pauses; can swim. *Manners :* Wary, commonest of all waders, gregarious in large flocks. Migrates by night and day. Near nests March-July. Cock scrapes false nests. In courtship, fights, bowings and flights. Hen works at scrapes after pairing. Cock flies off nest, hen runs and then flies. Feign injury. Young crouch. Mob Hawks, Crows and Partridges. In long flights, travel straight without ordered formation. Stamp for worms. Go to coast in frost.

DOTTEREL

LAPWING

TURNSTONE—*ARENARIA INTERPRES.*[2]

Length 9 ins. In winter, plumage darker and browner. *Female*, duller. *Passage* (July and May), some winter migrants. Go south along E. coast in autumn. Some remain in S. and W. *Nests* abroad. *Food :* Small marine life, picked from under weed and stones. " Tangle Picker." Young: larvæ of insects, attended by both parents. *Voice :* Short trill, long chuckling twitter. *Flight :* Rather wavering, wings arched, not fully extended. *Gait :* Walks ; can swim well. *Manners :* Exclusively seashore bird. Wader on rocks. Favourite spot, edge of waves. Tip over stones with bill and chest. Sometimes help each other.

OYSTER CATCHER—*HÆMATOPUS OSTRALE-GUS OCCIDENTALIS.*

Length 16½ ins. *Sexes* alike. In winter, sides of neck and half collar white. *Resident* on rocky coasts, chiefly W. and N., and some inland waters in Scotland ; also winter migrants. *Nests* (April-May) on rocks or shingle by sea ; 3-4 eggs, 1 brood. Male helps incubate, keeps guard and helps to guide young. *Food :* Shellfish (not oysters), sea worms, shrimps and crustacea. *Voice :* Shrill cry, "Kleep-kleep!" Alarm, "Pic Pic!" Piping, trilling nuptial song. *Flight :* Rapid, very straight, with regular beat of fully extended wings. *Gait :* Rapid trotting run. Swims easily. *Manners :* Very shy and wary. In autumn, form small flocks. In winter, south-ward movements. Crowd on reefs and islets. When tide falls they run out over the sand to catch limpets, etc., before they are closed. Males make false nests. Sometimes follow plough. In courtship, males pipe together before female.

TURNSTONE

OYSTER CATCHER

HERRING GULL—*LARUS ARGENTATUS.*[2]

Length 24 ins. *Sexes* alike. In winter, crown and neck streaked ash colour. *Resident* and common on all coasts of United Kingdom, except flat E. coast. Works southwards in winter. *Nests* (April-May) on rocky ledges at cliff head, grassy islands, shingle beds and moors ; 3 eggs, 1 brood reared. Male helps incubate and mounts guard. *Food :* Omnivorous ; worms, insects, crustacea, fish, garbage, grain, birds, voles, mice and eggs. Young, fed on regurgitated food by both parents. *Voice :* Loud, strident " Ki-ow ! "; deep threat, " Ha-ha-ha ! " *Flight :* Deliberate, powerful, controlled. Steers with tail. Drifts and sails. Swoops to pick up food, dipping head in water. *Gait :* Walks, stands on one leg, head to wind. Swims gracefully, rarely submerges. *Manners :* Gregarious. Follows plough. Tramples in shallow water. Feeds at tide line. Drops shellfish from height to crack them. Kills and guts Puffin chicks. Pellets. Young leave nests in few days and hide. Dashes down on intruders threatening to strike head.

LESSER BLACK-BACKED GULL—*LARUS FUSCUS BRITANNICUS.*

Length 23 ins. *Sexes* alike. In winter, crown and neck streaked ash colour. *Summer migrant,* on rocky cliffs and islands of United Kingdom. Rarely breeds in S.E. ; some residents. Moves southwards in winter. *Nests* (May) on tops of grass-covered islands, and moors inland, sometimes on cliffs ; 2-3 eggs, 1 brood reared. In other respects as Herring Gull, except more migratory and bolder.

NOTE.—The Scandinavian type (*L. f.*[3]), with blacker back, visits our coasts on passage and in winter.

HERRING GULL

LESSER BLACK-BACKED GULL

GREAT BLACK-BACKED GULL—*LARUS MARINUS.*

Length 30 ins. *Sexes* alike. *Resident* in Scotland and locally in Ireland and W. England. In winter spreads to South. *Nests* (early May) in inaccessible sites; 2-3 eggs, 1 brood reared. Differs from Herring Gull as follows:—Rarer and less gregarious. Greater strength allows it to prey on larger birds and wounded animals. "Vulture of the Sea." Strays to greater distance from land. Flight slower and voice deeper.

COMMON GULL—*LARUS CANUS.*[2]

Length 18½ ins. *Sexes* alike. In winter, head and neck streaked with brown; legs and feet pale brown. *Resident* in Scotland and W. Ireland. In winter, spreads to rest of United Kingdom. *Nests* (mid-May) on low grassy slopes, avoiding cliffs; 3 eggs, 1 brood reared. Differs from Herring Gull as follows: *Voice:* Usual call a sharp "Kak-kak-kak!"; also a loud "Kyah!" and many others. It steals fewer eggs, worms and insects being its chief food, though it is quite omnivorous. The name is a misnomer, the commonest Gull being the Black-Headed.

GREAT BLACK-BACKED GULL

COMMON GULL

BLACK-HEADED GULL–*LARUS RIDIBUNDUS.*[2]

Length 16 ins. *Sexes* alike. *Resident* and abundant on all flat sea-coasts and estuaries. *Nests* (April) inland, in thousands, in swampy ground, on sandhills or, rarely, in trees ; 3, rarely 4, eggs ; 1 brood reared. Male helps incubate. *Food :* Earthworms and insects, sometimes grain and fish. Young, insects and worms, disgorged by parents. *Voice :* Guttural, laughing "Kak!" Harsh scream when angry. *Flight and Gait :* As Herring Gull, but more rapid. *Manners :* Very noisy and gregarious. Generally as other Gulls, but commoner inland. Very bold when breeding. Menacing gestures, sometimes serious fights. Steals food from other birds when fishing. Commonest of all Gulls.

KITTIWAKE—*RISSA TRIDACTYLA.*[2]

Length 15½ ins. *Sexes* alike. In winter, head washed with grey. *Resident* on cliffs of W. Coasts, the Isles, Ireland, Man, Lundy, and a few places on N.E. coasts. Also *winter migrant. Nests* (May-June) on ledges of steep cliffs ; 2-3 eggs, 1 brood reared. Male helps build, incubate and feed. *Food :* Chiefly small fish and ova, surface crustacea. *Voice :* "Kittiwaake!" *Flight, Gait and Manners :* Generally as other Gulls, but more maritime. Has followed ships across Atlantic. Affectionate, rather silent. In feeding, hovers, then dashes down on water with great force. Skilful diver. Does not regurgitate, but allows young to fish in its mouth. Many killed in gales.

BLACK-HEADED GULL
Summer and Winter (Head)

KITTIWAKE

COMMON TERN—*STERNA HIRUNDO.*[2]

Length 14¼ ins. *Sexes* alike. *Summer migrant*, April-Oct. on shores throughout United Kingdom, rarer northwards. *Nests*, or merely *lays* (June), on bare rocks, shingle beds, mud flats or meadow grass; 2-3 eggs, 1 brood reared. Eggs left uncovered for long periods in the sun. Male helps feed. *Food :* Small fish and crustacea ; insects on fresh waters. *Voice :* Harsh screaming, " Pirre ! " ; also " Kit-kit ! " *Flight :* Beats over sea with slow powerful strokes. Hovers, with wings vibrating high, beak and tail pointing downwards. Then closes wings and dives for food, rising instantaneously. *Gait :* Walks little and badly. Swims easily, but slowly. *Manners :* Sea bird, only found on fresh water when migrating. Breeds in communities. Male feeds female in courtship (struts round her, head and tail high, fish dangling from beak, until his overtures are accepted) and when incubating. Bold in defence of nest, striking at a man's head with beak and killing intruding birds and beasts.

ARCTIC TERN—*STERNA MACRURA.*

Length 14½ ins. *Sexes* alike. *Summer migrant*, Apl.-Oct., in Scotland and Ireland, locally in England and Wales. Differs from Common Tern as follows : Breeds later in June, preferring island sites. Its call is shorter, a harsh " Kleeah ! " Sometimes eats earthworms.

COMMON TERN

ARCTIC TERN

ROSEATE TERN—*STERNA DOUGALLII.*[2]

Length 15½ ins. *Sexes* alike. *Summer migrant*, end April to end August, rare and local throughout United Kingdom coasts. Differs from Common Tern as follows :—*Lays* (late June) in bare hollows on rocks and on stacks, with other Terns ; 1-2 eggs. *Voice :* Recorded as " Chew-it ! " ; alarm, sharp " Aaack ! "

SANDWICH TERN—*STERNA SANDVICENSIS.*[2]

Length 16 ins. *Sexes* alike. *Summer migrant*, March to September, locally throughout coasts of United Kingdom. Differs from Common Tern as follows : Breeds in early May, usually on sand-dunes or sandy shores. Rarely lines nests, and then thinly. *Voice :* More musical, " Kirr-whit ! " Alarm, a sharp " Wheet ! " *Flight :* In hovering, tail not depressed, and when diving, longer submerged. The young ramble when only a few days old and scrape out hollows in sand for concealment. Nests are often very close together.

ROSEATE TERN

SANDWICH TERN

LITTLE TERN—*STERNA ALBIFRONS.*[2]

Length 9 ins. *Sexes* alike. *Summer migrant*, early May to September, throughout coasts of United Kingdom. Differs from Common Tern as follows : Breeds (mid-May) in small colonies with nests wide apart, rarely lines nest. *Lays* in depression in shingle in association, often, with Ringed Plovers. In *Flight*, wings beat quicker. *Voice :* Recorded as " Pee-e-err ! " " Zit-zit ! " and alarm, " Ki-ki-ki ! "

BLACK TERN—*CHLIDONIAS NIGER.*[2]

Length 9½ ins. *Female* rather lighter beneath. In winter, forehead, throat, nape and under parts white, which wears off with the feather tips. *Passage migrant* (April-June and July-Sept.) chiefly across S.E. England. Now obsolete as resident. *Nests* abroad. *Food :* Insects, taken in flight in air or from surface of water. Perhaps tadpoles and small fish. *Voice :* Silent in United Kingdom. *Flight :* Even more buoyant than other Terns, swoops and hovers. *Gait :* Walks, seldom swims. *Manners :* Sociable, in small flocks, sometimes with other Terns. Frequents fresh water more than salt. A Marsh Tern. Settles on posts, head low. Seldom or never dives.

LITTLE TERN

BLACK TERN

GREAT SKUA—*CATHARACTA SKUA.*[2]

Length 25 ins. *Sexes* alike. *Resident* in Shetlands and Orkneys. *Nests* (mid-May) on high moors; 2 eggs, 1 brood reared. Male helps incubate and feed. *Food :* Fish, crustacea, offal, carcases, small live birds, rodents and eggs. Pellets. *Voice :* In flight, a deep gull note ; during the chase, " Skua ! " ; alarm, angry bark. *Flight :* Gull-like, drifting, aimless, till it sees a bird with food, then, swift, relentless, dodging pursuit until the victim disgorges, when it " stoops " at the fish in the air. *Gait :* Walks. *Manners :* Solitary. " Robber Bird." On high sea from autumn to March-April, rarely coming to land. Pursues Terns, Gannets and all Gulls. In courtship, raises wings and postures. In defence of nests will fiercely and repeatedly attack, silently, striking with feet. Young fed by regurgitation.

ARCTIC SKUA—*STERCORARIUS PARASITICUS.*

Length 20 ins. *Sexes* alike. Varies greatly in colour. Dark and light types. *Resident* in N. Scotland and the Isles ; also passage migrant further S. Differs from Great Skua as follows :—Much more numerous ; gregarious, but nests widely separated. *Voice :* A plaintive " Mee ! " or " Mee-awh ! " Has been seen feeding on land and following the plough. In defence of nest usually attacks from behind and also feigns disablement Makes less, if any, nest.

GREAT SKUA

ARCTIC SKUA

RAZORBILL—*ALCA TORDA*.

Length 17 ins. *Sexes* alike. In winter, sides of head, throat and foreneck, white; line to eye, faint. *Resident* Mar-Aug. on cliffs, rest of year at sea. *Lays* (mid-May) 1 egg in cranny or on overhung ledge high on rocky cliff; 1 brood reared. Male helps incubate and feed. Egg lies on feet. *Food:* Small fish and crustacea. Drinks salt water. Young fed on fish, carried, several at a time, across bill. *Voice:* Low, guttural cry. Alarmed, low moaning. Rather silent. *Flight:* Rapid, in a line, almost touching, with head and tail low. *Gait:* Shuffles, sometimes hops, resting on shanks. Swims high, tail cocked. Dives quickly, swims under water with wings, steering with legs. *Manners:* Lives with Guillemots and Puffins. Pairs for life. Returns to old nest. In courtship, rub bills, nibble at plumage. In fights, fence with open bills. Breed in colonies, lining cliffs, face to sea. Sit on water in flocks at cliff foot. Gales wash many dead ashore. After 3 or 4 weeks, young are jostled down to water by parents, while still unable to fly.

GUILLEMOT—*URIA AALGE ALBIONIS.*

Length 18 ins. *Sexes* alike. In winter, sides of head, throat and upper foreneck, white; dark triangular patch backward from eye. Differs from Razorbill as follows:—More numerous. *Lays* on bare open shelf of rock. Carries only one fish, held lengthwise, to young. Noisier. Sitting bird more upright. Swims with tail low. Odd bowing movements in courtship.

NOTE.—The Northern type, breeding from the Shetlands northwards (*U. a.*²), is said to be darker. Winter migrant.

RAZORBILL

GUILLEMOT

BLACK GUILLEMOT—*URIA GRYLLE.*[2]

Length 14 ins. *Sexes* alike. In winter, underparts and rump white; feathers of back, head and neck, edged white. *Resident*, Feb.-Aug., on rocky coasts of N.W. Scotland, Ireland and the Isles. *Lays* (end May) 2-3 eggs in rock crevices, low, near sea; 1 brood reared. Male helps incubate and feed. *Food:* Crustacea, small fish, molluscs and seaweed. Young: as Guillemot. *Flight:* As Razorbill. *Voice:* Whining cry. Whistles in courtship. *Gait:* As Razorbill but more agile; can walk on toes. Rests on shanks; lies prone in incubation. *Manners:* As Razorbill, but young stay on rock till able to fly. Scarcer, groups rarely exceed 60.

PUFFIN—*FRATERCULA ARCTICA GRABÆ.*

Length 12 ins. *Sexes* alike. In moult, sheds blue parts from beak and eye. *Resident* and summer migrant, chiefly cliffs, throughout United Kingdom. Great numbers in N. and W. *Nests* (mid-May) in burrows dug in turf near cliff tops. Sometimes ejects rabbit. Male helps dig, incubate and feed; 1 egg, 1 brood reared. *Food:* As Razorbill. *Voice:* Deep grumbling " Arrr ! " Very silent, often opens beak silently. *Flight:* Runs with quivering wings, slowly rising. Feet gathered up, soles together, in the air, but trailed backwards when diving. Swift, vibrating. *Gait:* Stands, walks, and runs swiftly on toes. Under water as Razorbill. *Manners:* As Razorbill. Fights fiercely for holes. Many non-breeders.

BLACK GUILLEMOT
(Summer and Winter)

PUFFIN

STORMY PETREL—*THALASSIDROMA PELAGICA.*

Length 6½ ins. Square tail. *Sexes* alike. *Resident* in British waters. *Nests* (June) in colonies, in holes in walls and loose stones or old rabbit burrows, all up W. coast on remote islands; 1 egg. Both sexes incubate. *Food :* Small crustacea, cephalopods, small fish, and when nesting, sorrel. Young fed on regurgitated oil skimmed off water. *Voice :* When nesting, husky; noisy at night, silent on water. *Flight :* Buoyant, skimming, swift, Tern-like, erratic. Often glides along water, paddling with feet. Dips head to surface to pick up food. *Gait :* Cannot stand, rests and shuffles on shanks, rising with help of wings. Swims on roughest sea. *Manners :* Oceanic. Comes to land only to breed in April or May, or if storm-driven. Follows ships for crustacea. Squirts oil from bill if handled. Smallest web-footed bird. When breeding, nocturnal.

LEACH'S PETREL—*OCEANODROMA LEUCORRHOA.*[2]

Differs from Stormy Petrel in the following respects : Larger, 8¼ ins. Forked tail. *Nests* in a few Scottish and Irish Islands, in holes dug 2-3 ft. deep in peaty soil. Much rarer.

STORMY PETREL

LEACH'S PETREL

MANX SHEARWATER—*PUFFINUS.*[3]

Length 15 ins. *Sexes* alike. *Resident* on islands off
W. and N. coasts, and one or two places mainland.
Southward migration, Aug.-Sept. *Nests* (May) in
colonies, in burrows, caves or among rocks ; 1 egg.
Both sexes burrow, feed and incubate. Young fed on
regurgitated oil. *Food :* As Stormy Petrel. *Voice :*
Harsh, scolding ; soft crooning when breeding.
Noisy at night, specially after rain. *Flight :* Un-
hurried glide. Shears wavetops, leaning over to
alternate sides. When travelling, flies swifter and
straighter, with slow strokes. Rises with difficulty
from shore. *Gait :* As Stormy Petrel. Rests flat on
breast and shanks. Dives for a few seconds.
Manners : Lives on open sea except when breeding
(Feb. to end of summer) when one bird goes to sea to
forage. Migrations cross land, dropping stragglers.

FULMAR—*FULMARUS GLACIALIS.*[2]

Length 19 ins. *Sexes* alike. *Resident* on British seas,
widespread in winter, increasing. *Nests* or *lays* (mid-
May) in shallow hole on cliffs of the Isles, Yorkshire,
Scotland and N. and W. Ireland ; 1 egg. Both sexes
incubate and feed. *Food :* Fish, oily refuse, cuttles
and, on land, sorrel. Young, as Stormy Petrel.
Voice : Silent. Grunts when displaying; low crooning
when nesting. *Flight :* As Shearwater, sweeping in
huge arcs. *Gait :* Alights on water feet first and sinks
with open wings. *Manners :* Oceanic wanderer, on
land only for breeding (May-August). Follows ships.
Tame. After pairing, grotesque antics. When
brooding, mother resents approach of mate with oil
squirting. Excrement ejected away from nest.

MANX SHEARWATER

FULMAR

BLACK-THROATED DIVER—*COLYMBUS ARCTICUS.*[2]

Length 28 ins. Winter dress, uniform dark brown above with few white spots on wing coverts; throat and under parts white. *Sexes* alike. *Resident* in small numbers on N. and W. coasts of Scotland and the Isles. Winter migrant to most coasts, sometimes inland. *Nests* or *lays* (end May) on withered grass near coast, and on islands in mountain lochs; 2 eggs, 1 brood. Both sexes incubate and feed. *Food :* Fish (mostly trout and parr), some molluscs and vegetable matter. Large fish killed on surface. Wipes bill and sips after diving. *Voice :* Variety of harsh cries and yelps in flight and when breeding. Madman's laugh. *Flight :* Rise flapping along water, cannot rise from land. Fly in line with outstretched neck and trailed legs. Descend obliquely. *Gait :* Scramble on breast swiftly with feet and wings. Swim low, alternate strokes. Under water, simultaneous strokes, sometimes wings also. Dive with regular "header," or lowering neck and gliding under. Long dives. Rise cautiously. *Manners :* Found on salt and fresh water, sometimes in numbers. Pair on nest. Nestlings carried on back. Bold when with young. Often upright on water, flapping wings.

GREAT NORTHERN DIVER—*COLYMBUS IMMER.*[2]

Length 31 ins. Winter dress, upper part dark brown, each feather edged ash, wing coverts unspotted. *Sexes* alike. *Winter migrant*, chiefly to W. coasts. Passage on all coasts. *Nests* abroad. Differs from Black-Throated as follows :—No evidence of vegetable food. Usually seen solitary.

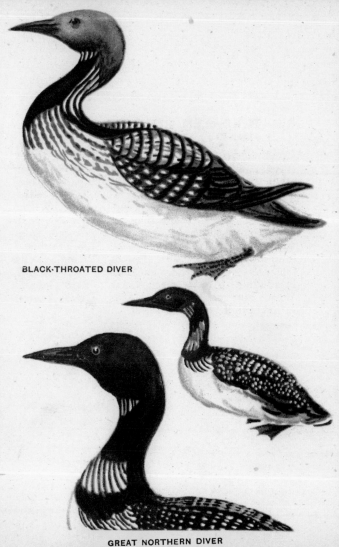

BLACK-THROATED DIVER

GREAT NORTHERN DIVER

RED-THROATED DIVER—*COLYMBUS STELLATUS.*

Length 25 ins. In winter, loses red throat and neck stripes; all upper parts slatey grey, marked with white spots; flanks slatey grey; under parts, including cheeks, chin and throat, white. *Sexes* alike. *Resident* in W. and N. Scotland and the Isles. Winter migrant to all our coasts (mid-September to April). Much more numerous than Black-Throated, from whom it differs as follows:—*Nest:* More substantial (mid-May). *Food:* More oceanic. Young: chiefly sand eels. *Voice:* Has a loud bark, " Kark Kark ! " in addition to other divers cries. " Rain Goose." When not scared, floats higher. Dives shorter. More upright on land.

RED-THROATED DIVER

GREAT CRESTED GREBE—*PODICEPS CRISTATUS.*[2]

Length 21 ins. Crest erectile, no tail. In winter loses frill and part of ears. *Sexes* alike. *Resident* on lakes of United Kingdom, rare in Highlands and S.W. Rapidly increasing. *Nests* (April-May) among reeds, on floating mass of decaying weeds ; 3-4 eggs, sometimes 2 broods. Both sexes build, incubate and feed, each assuming all care of certain chicks. *Food :* Fish, newts, insects and vegetation. Young, fed on small fish. Feathers eaten for digestion. *Voice :* Usually silent except when breeding. " Jick Jick Jick ! " and harsh croak. *Flight :* Duck-like, neck drooped, head and feet outstretched. *Gait :* Walks little but easily, on feet. Swims, feet outwards, low in water ; neck usually vertical, thrust forward at speed ; when resting, head on back. Dives for speed, gliding under. Under water, swims with lateral simultaneous strokes. *Manners :* Flock (Oct.) and migrate (Nov.) to sea, returning Feb. Pair end Feb. and remain in families till Oct. Feed by day. Rarely fly except courting. Before and after pairing (which occurs on nest), both sexes, in displaying, erect ruffs, shake heads, preen, raise wings, revolve and dance, breast to breast, on water. Eggs covered before leaving nest. Carry young on back. Often build near Coots.

NOTE.—The "British Birds" census of 1931 found 2,650 adults in Great Britain, against 42 breeding pairs in 1860.

RED-NECKED GREBE—*PODICEPS GRISEIGENA.*[2]

Length 18 ins. In winter loses part of ears. *Sexes* alike. *Winter* visitor in small numbers. Differs from Great Crested as follows :—*Nests* abroad. Confined to salt water in winter. Walks more easily.

GREAT CRESTED GREBE

RED-NECKED GREBE

SLAVONIAN GREBE—*PODICEPS AURITUS.*

Length 13½ ins. In winter, loses all red colour and
has white cheeks. *Sexes* alike. *Winter migrant* and
passage on most coasts. Some residents in N.
Scotland. Differs from Great Crested as follows:
Chiefly frequents calm waters. Swims higher in
water. Flies more readily and with neck horizontal.
Dives very quickly and for a short period. Eggs
laid in June.

BLACK-NECKED GREBE—*PODICEPS NIGRI-COLLIS.*[2]

Length 12 ins. In winter, under parts white except
for dusky band on neck, upper parts brownish-black.
Female smaller and ears less marked. *Winter migrant*
and passage. Some summer visitors. Establishing
itself as resident in Wales. Swims buoyantly
unless alarmed, otherwise like the Dabchick.

SLAVONIAN GREBE

BLACK-NECKED GREBE

DABCHICK—*PODICEPS RUFICOLLIS.*[2]

Length 10 ins. Marked seasonal change. *Sexes* alike. *Resident* throughout the United Kingdom, in summer, in all slow-flowing inland waters, on larger lakes in winter and, in severe weather, on coasts. *Nests* (end April) among reeds, on floating mass of decaying weeds ; 4-6 eggs, 2 broods. Second nest for later brood. Both sexes build, incubate and feed. Heat of nest helps hatch eggs. *Food :* Water insects, small fish, tadpoles, weeds and feathers (for digestion). *Voice :* Short, subdued, whistling call. Rippling trill down the scale. *Flight :* Flies often, with quick fluttering short wings. *Gait :* Runs very swiftly, on toes. Swims with neck curved back, alternate strokes. Dives, sometimes jumping up and with squirt of water backwards, sometimes silently. Swims under water with feet only, lateral and simultaneous strokes. Regains surface cautiously, showing bill only. *Manners :* Very active. When alarmed covers eggs with weeds and dives. Hides in weeds with bill alone shewing. Carries young on back.

DABCHICK
(Summer and Winter)

CORNCRAKE—*CREX*.[2]

Length 11 ins. *Female* has grey feathers paler. In winter the grey is replaced by ochre and flanks are barred dark brown. *Summer migrant*, mid-April-May to Aug.-Oct., throughout United Kingdom, chiefly W. and N. Some few residents. *Nests* (mid-May) in depression in pasture or weeds ; 8-12, up to 18, eggs ; 1-2 broods. Male does not build or incubate. *Food :* Mainly insects, some seeds. Swallows grit. Young fed by female for 4 days, then guided by both parents. *Voice :* Loud, rasping, monotonous "Crake !" till June. When fighting, angry grunt. Call, a weak hen-like cackle. *Flight :* Flies only if pressed ; laborious, with drooping legs, dropping at first cover. *Gait :* Walks high stepping, with head bobbing. Alarmed, runs swiftly, with head low, outstretched. Sometimes swims. *Manners :* Solitary, migrate singly or in pairs at night. Fight fiercely for chosen ground. Courtship similar to domestic fowls. Autumn moult very rapid. Dust bathers. Rarely perch. Sham dead.

SPOTTED CRAKE—*PORZANA*.[2]

Length 9 ins. *Sexes* alike. *Summer migrant*, March-Oct., and passage. Rare and local, chiefly S.E. Differs from Corncrake as follows :—*Nests* in tussocks in inland waters. Male helps incubate. *Food :* Insects, molluscs, seeds. *Voice :* Cock in courtship, "Tric Trec !" Swims as Moorhen. *Flies* even more reluctantly, but better, somewhat as Starling. Even shyer and more secretive. Will hide under water, holding to a rush.

214

CORNCRAKE

SPOTTED CRAKE

WATER RAIL—*RALLUS AQUATICUS.*[2]

Length 11½ ins. *Sexes* alike. *Resident* except in the
Isles and Highlands, chiefly in E. Anglia and Ireland;
also winter migrants. *Nests* (early April) in tussocks
in marshes; 6-12 eggs, 2 broods. Male helps
incubate and feed young; also feeds female. *Food:*
Worms, snails, slugs, small fish and some vegetables.
Voice: Loud explosive groaning call; also a contented purring sound, and "Chiff Chuff!" *Flight
and Gait:* As Corncrake. Swims rapidly and dives
with ease. *Manners:* Extremely shy, silent and
furtive. Frequents fens, marshes and water-courses.
Young, fed by regurgitation for some time and then
guided by both parents. In courtship male preens
female's feathers. Fights a Gull by lying on its back.

MOORHEN—*GALLINULA CHLOROPUS.*[2]

Length 13 ins. *Sexes* alike. *Resident* and common
throughout United Kingdom, on all inland waters.
Drifts south in winter. *Nests* (Apr.) near water among
rushes or in hedges, bushes or trees. Sometimes uses
other birds' nests. Several nests built and used for
brooding; 6-10 eggs, 2-3 broods. Male helps build
(at night), incubate and feed young. Earlier broods
feed the later. *Food:* Almost omnivorous, chiefly
vegetable. *Flight:* As Corncrake. *Gait:* Runs
swiftly, bobbing head and jerking tail. Swims with
bobbing head. Dives, and, under water, swims with
legs and wings. *Voice:* Sudden "Prruk!" at night,
and migrating, "Kik Kik Kik!" *Manners:* Not
very shy. Pugnacious. Fights as Game Cock.
Hides under water. Courting males spin round in
water with tails outspread.

WATER RAIL

MOORHEN

COOT—*FULICA ATRA.*[2]

Length 18 ins. *Sexes* alike. *Resident* and common throughout United Kingdom on large sheets of water inland. Slow rivers and marshes. Rare in Shetlands. Drifts south in winter. *Nests* (mid-March to May) among reeds in the water. Male helps build, incubate and feed young; 7-9 eggs, probably 2 broods. *Food :* Water plants ; also insects and molluscs, grain and grass, berries and worms. Young: water plants. *Voice :* A clear loud "Honk ! " also a sharp clinking sound. *Flight :* Slow riser, paddling and flapping on water. Once clear, straight and fairly strong, with feet under tail. Feet stretched down to alight. *Gait :* Walks and runs easily. Swims with bobbing head and alternate leg-strokes. Dives, turning over with a jump. Under water, swims with simultaneous leg-strokes and wings folded. *Manners :* More aquatic than Moorhen, seldom seen on land. Seldom flies unless disturbed or to chase another bird. Gregarious in winter. Hides under water as Moorhen. Less tame than Moorhen, but not very shy. Brings weed to surface to eat ; also beats weeds with foot to dislodge insects. Quarrel over territory. Roost by nest in breeding season, in bushes and trees at other times. Hard frost drives them to sea.

COOT

WOOD PIGEON—*COLUMBA PALUMBUS.*[2]

Length 17 ins. *Sexes* alike. *Resident* and winter migrant (end Oct.-Feb.), throughout United Kingdom in wooded districts. *Nests* (early April) high in trees, often in old nests of other birds and squirrels; 2-3 eggs, 1-3 broods. Male alone brings material and helps build, incubate and feed. *Food:* Grain, peas, beechmast, acorns, nuts, berries, clover and turnips. Young put bills into bill of parent and take "milk" pumped up from walls of crop, later mixed with half-digested food. *Voice:* "Coo-roo-coo-coo!" from Mar. (sometimes Jan.) to Oct. *Flight:* Regular, swift and powerful. *Gait:* Walks, waddling. *Manners:* Monogamous. Drink freely. Roost in large numbers. Fly head to wind. Gregarious in winter. Crops can hold 60 acorns. In courtship, male walks along bough or ground, bowing, cooing, and raising tail; also aerial circling displays. "Ring Dove."

STOCK DOVE—*COLUMBA ŒNAS.*

Length 13½ ins. *Sexes* alike. *Resident*, local, throughout United Kingdom, spreading from S.E. Parks, open country, sand dunes. Winter migrants. *Lays* (April) in hole in tree or rock, rabbit burrow or squirrel drey; 2-3 eggs, 2-3 broods. Male helps incubate and feed. *Food:* As *Palumbus. Voice:* Grunting "Coo!" mostly while breeding. *Flight:* Lighter and more rapid than *Palumbus. Gait:* Walks and runs, bobbing. *Manners:* Perches well, drinks freely, tyrannical to female. Associates with *Palumbus.* Courtship as *Palumbus*, but more silent.

WOOD PIGEON

STOCK DOVE

ROCK DOVE—*COLUMBA LIVIA*.[2]

Length 13½ ins. *Sexes* alike. *Resident* and stationary on cliff coasts of Yorks., Devon, Cornwall, Wales, Cumberland, Scotland and Ireland. *Nests* (April) on a rock ledge or in caves; 2 eggs, several broods. Male feeds female and young, and occasionally incubates. *Food*: Grain, seeds and roots of weeds. Young: "milk." *Voice*: Dovecot "Coo!" most vociferous during breeding season. *Flight*: Strong and swift, flying low over water. *Gait*: Walks and runs. *Manners*: Never lights on trees. Drinks freely sometimes alighting on water. Tyrannical to female. Gregarious. Courtship same as *Palumbus*. Domestic Pigeons bred from Rock Dove. Interbreeds with them.

TURTLE DOVE--*STREPTOPELIA TURTUR*.[2]

Length 11½ ins. *Sexes* alike. *Summer migrant* (end April-Sept.) to S. and E. England; also passage in other districts. Open woods and plantations. *Nests* (end May) low in tree or hedgerow; 2 eggs, 2 broods. Male helps bring material, incubate and feed. *Food*: Grain, small seeds, berries and small molluscs. Young: "milk." *Voice*: Low plaintive "Coo-rrr!" heard irregularly for a week after arrival and then regularly until early Aug. *Flight*: Powerful, tortuous among trees. Wings clapped sharply together. *Gait*: Walks with easy steps. *Manners*: Generally like *Palumbus*. Pugnacious, less gregarious but flocks in autumn. In courtship, bobs repeatedly instead of slowly bowing; when on ground, hops between bobs. All pigeons will drink salt water.

ROCK DOVE

TURTLE DOVE

PHEASANT—*PHASIANUS COLCHICUS.*

(Plate represents hybrid between *Colchicus* and *Torquatus*, now the almost universal type). Length, with tail, 36 ins. *Hen* smaller, brown, shorter tail, no spur. *Resident* throughout United Kingdom in wood and thick cover. First imported by the Romans and generally " reared." *Nests* (April) in hollow in cover; 10-14 eggs, 1 brood. Cock does not incubate. *Food :* Roots, grain, berries, acorns, wireworms, insects, vipers and mice. Young feed on insects, accompanied by hen. *Voice :* Cock crows and then flaps wings. Loud rattling sound when rising and roosting. *Flight :* Laborious, whirring, but swift. *Gait :* Walks and runs swiftly; also can swim. Roosts in trees. Otherwise a ground bird. Feeds on arable and pasture. When alarmed, crouches, rising only when obliged. *Manners :* Fights as Gamecock. Polygamous. In courting, runs around hen trailing wings. Needs thick cover and water to thrive. Flies to and from nest.

RED-LEGGED PARTRIDGE—*ALECTORIS RUFA.*[2]

Length 13½ ins. *Hen*, no spur. *Resident* S. and mid-England. Imported 1770. Dry wasteland, commons, sandy soil. *Nests* (April-May) on ground, sometimes on a stack; 15-18 eggs, 1 brood. Hen alone builds and incubates. *Voice :* Clear musical piping call, " Chuk-chuk-chuk-er ! " *Food, Flight, Gait and Manners :* Very wild, sometimes perches on trees or rails. Avoids flying if possible. When disturbed, coveys scatter. Otherwise resembles Partridge.

PHEASANT

RED-LEGGED PARTRIDGE

PARTRIDGE—*PERDIX*.[3]

Length 12½ ins. *Hen* has minor plumage differences including black wing-coverts with wavy buff crossbars and shaft-streaks. Both sexes have "eclipse" plumage of head and neck (May-Sept.) *Resident* on all low-lying land. *Nests* (Apr.-May) in scratched-out hollow in hedgerows, under bush or bank-side; 10-20 eggs, 1 brood. Hen alone incubates, cock keeping watch. *Food:* Grass, clover, heather, bramble, blueberry, spiders, insects. Young feed themselves on insects and larvæ, accompanied by both parents. *Voice:* Clucking alarm note. *Flight:* Whirring, heavy, rapid, rising just high enough to clear hedges. Skims to earth with decurved wings. *Gait:* Runs swiftly. *Manners:* Pugnacious, monogamous. When cocks fight, hen runs round the pair. Never perches except in case of deep snow. Dust bather, sometimes water bather. Live in coveys. When disturbed keep together. Sleep in open. Feed morning and evening, quiet between. Gallant in defence of young; feign injury. In February coveys break up and courting begins.

QUAIL—*COTURNIX*.[3]

Length 7 ins. *Hen* lacks black neck markings. *Summer migrant* (May-Oct.), occasionally wintering in S. England and E. Ireland. Rough pastures and arable, usually wheat field. *Nests* (end May) in hollow scratched in growing crops; 7-14 eggs, 1 "bevy." Cock does not incubate. *Food and Gait:* As Partridge. *Voice:* Cock, "Wet-my-lips!" Hen, "Piou-piou!" *Flight:* As Partridge, but shorter. *Manners:* Wary. Dust bather. Gregarious migrant. Cocks arrive first. Stake out claims. Fight fiercely.

PARTRIDGE

QUAIL

CAPERCAILLIE—*TETRAO UROGALLUS.*[2]

Length 34 ins. "Eclipse" dress in summer. *Hen* 23 ins., as GreyHen but round red tail. *Resident* in Scotland. Forests, mainly pine. Re-introduced 1837. *Nests* (end April) in hollow scratched by hen at foot of tree; 6-8 eggs, up to 15; 1 brood. Hen alone incubates. *Food:* Buds, insects, berries, acorns, grain and fir shoots. Young eat worms and insects, accompanied by hen. *Voice:* Cock's call, "Peller Peller!" Hen feeding in winter calls "Kok Kok!" *Flight:* As Pheasant. *Gait:* Walks. *Manners:* Polygamous. Inter-breeds with Grey Hen. Roosts and sits in tree-tops. In spring, cocks fight fiercely and, at dawn, perform a "spel" (frenzied dance with wild, excited song), each in a favourite tree. Hens collect to admire. Hen devoted mother, covers nest with pine needles when leaving to feed. In severe weather seek valleys. Burrow in snow.

BLACK COCK & GREY HEN—*LYRURUS*
TETRIX BRITANNICUS.

Length 22 ins. "Eclipse" dress of head and back. *Hen* 18 ins., forked grey tail. *Resident* in Scotland, Wales, N. and S.W. England. Woods and rough land near moors. *Nests* (May) in scratched-out hollow in wood or open; 6-10 eggs, up to 16; 1 brood. Hen alone incubates. *Voice:* Hoarse and powerful. *Food, Flight, Gait and Manners:* Generally as Caper. Also breeds with Grouse and sometimes Pheasant. In courtship, cocks gather in open space and fight, in presence of hens, at dawn. Dance in intervals. ("Lek") Hen is careless mother. Assemble end Sept. in the open.

CAPERCAILLIE

BLACK COCK & GREY HEN

GROUSE—*LAGOPUS SCOTICUS.*[2]

Length 16 ins. *Hen* smaller and lighter in colour. "Eclipse" dress, cock June, hen Mar.-Oct. Coloration varies much. *Resident* in Wales, Yorkshire, Pennines, Scotland and Ireland. Moor and mountain. *Nests* (April-May) in heather or rough grass; 7-12 eggs, 1 brood. Cock does not incubate. *Food:* Heather, ling, crowberry, seeds, grain and berries. Young feed on caterpillars, insects and young shoots, accompanied by both parents. *Flight:* As Partridge, but longer. *Gait:* Walks and runs. *Voice:* "Kok-kok-kok!" on rising, "Go-back Goback Goback!" on alighting. Hen, odd nasal croak. *Manners:* Monogamous. Dust bather. In courtship, cocks fight. The victor rises to height of 20 feet, crowing. Descends and takes chosen hen away. Hen sits close. Both parents will defend young. Coveys pack in hard weather and go to valleys. Said to burrow under snow. Coveys break up in March. Sheds claws in moult. The only exclusively British species. It has, however, been recently exported.

NOTE.—Irish and O. Hebridean birds (*L. s. hibernicus*) are slightly paler in winter.

PTARMIGAN—*LAGOPUS MUTUS MILLAISI.*

Length 15 ins. Changes dress April (as plate); August (bluer and paler); November (pure white except for red comb over eye and black stripes round eye and outside tail). *Hen,* when coloured, browner and lighter. *Resident* in Scotland, on mountains over 2,000 ft. *Nests* (end May) in scratched-out hollow in moss; 7-12 eggs, 1 brood. Cock does not incubate. *Food:* Shoots and fruits of plants. Young feed on grass shoots and blaeberry leaves, broken up for them by parents. *Voice:* Low croak, delivered perched on stone. *Flight:* Strongest of any game bird. *Gait and Manners:* Generally as Grouse. Roosts in snow. Chief foes, Eagle, Fox and Gulls (who eat their eggs).

GROUSE

PTARMIGAN

EGGS

Eggs differ greatly from each other in size, shape, texture and colour. Those of the same species, even of the same bird in the same clutch, vary greatly. The expert can usually name the layer from the egg alone, as a bank clerk knows his customer's signature, but pictures of one egg for each bird are misleading and verbal descriptions, without plates, not very helpful. Here I wish to give a few general ideas.

VARIATION.—Many species lay eggs of very various shapes, sizes and colour. The Black-Throated Diver's egg can be the longest in shape of all eggs, or again can be the shape of that of a hen. The Sparrow's varies greatly in both shape and size (see *p.* 233). As to colour, it is the exception rather than the rule not to vary. The most notably variable are those of the Cuckoo, Tree Pipit, Sparrow, Grouse, Crows, Rook, Yellow Hammer, the Larks, Gulls, Terns and, above all, of the Guillemot.

The following are all Cuckoos' eggs :—

EGGS

These three are Tree Pipits' :—

And these four, Sparrows' :—

The uniform eggs (what the linen drapers call "self-coloured") vary little, as do those of the Lesser Whitethroat, the Tits, Reed Bunting, Goldfinch and the Grey Hen.

SIZE.—As a rule, the size of the bird governs that of the egg, but those whose young leave the nest early, and those which lay few eggs, tend to have the larger eggs. Striking examples of birds laying

NOTE.—All these plates were drawn from eggs in the B.M. collection and are of natural size. The Cuckoos' eggs, respectively in order, are from the nests of a Meadow Pipit, Brambling, Yellow Wagtail, Yellow Hammer and Meadow Pipit.

large eggs are the Puffin, the Guillemot and the Snipe, whose eggs are as large as those of the domestic Hen, the Eagle and the Rook respectively. On the other hand the Cuckoo's egg (see illustration) is very small.

SHAPE.—A bird's egg is always spherical when it leaves the ovary, and its final form when laid (the white, the shell and the colour, if any, having been added in the oviduct) is the result of the downward squeezing which the sphere receives in that passage. The larger end comes first. An egg (viewed from the side) is rarely a regular oval or ellipse. In the great majority of cases one end has a half circle for its outline, the other an ellipse more or less pointed. But many birds, which nest on open ground or on rock ledges, lay pointed eggs which either pack closely, point to point, under the mother, or will not roll, because the sides are straight lines joining the large round end to the small elliptical point. Striking examples of this are found among the eggs of the Plovers and other Waders, and of the Guillemot and Razorbill. But for this shape, the Snipe could hardly cover her large eggs.

Of the eggs of normal type (*i.e.*, circle and ellipse) some are nearly spherical, *e.g.*, those of the Owls, the Hawks, the Kingfisher and (usually) the Woodcock. Others are notably long or elliptical at both ends, such as those of the Grebes and (usually) the Divers.

The Nightjar (see *p.* 238) is one of the few birds whose egg is almost a perfect oval.

TEXTURE.—The surface of eggs varies from the smooth glazed china of the Thrush, the Kingfisher or the Woodpeckers to the rough plaster of the Swift, Gannet, Cormorant and Shag.

COLOUR.—The colour, if any, is put upon the shell from minute openings in the oviduct shortly before the egg is laid. It clearly often serves as camouflage in exposed situations, and may also help to protect the embryo from the rays of the sun. Eggs laid in the dark are safer from damage by the bird itself, if visible, and all eggs so laid are white or nearly white.* The converse rule that all white eggs are laid in the dark is true only of the small birds.†

The main distinction is between eggs of uniform colour, without markings, and those marked with darker colours.

UNIFORM EGGS.—The following is a complete list of the birds which lay eggs of one colour only. Several more species do so very exceptionally, but these I have not included.

Pure White : The Dipper, House and Sand Martins, all Woodpeckers, Wryneck, Swift, Kingfisher, and, of the large birds, all the Owls, the Cormorant, Shag, Gannet, Fulmar, Sheldrake, and all the Doves.

* NOTE.—The Tits' and Nuthatch's are the only eggs marked at all, except the Puffin's, which are marked, but smeared with white.

† NOTE.—Most of the large birds which lay white or whitish eggs in the open, either rarely leave them or cover them when they do.

Greenish White: All the Geese, Swans, Ducks (except the Sheldrake) and Grebes. Those of the Teal and Widgeon are yellowish rather than greenish.

Pale Khaki: The Pheasant, Partridge and Bittern.

Olive Green: The Nightingale.

Blue (very pale): The Wheatear, Stonechat, Pied Flycatcher and Starling; (less pale) the Whinchat, Redstart, Hedge Sparrow; and, of the large birds, the Heron and (very pale) the Harriers. Of the above, the Stonechat's egg is generally, and the Whinchat's often, faintly marked with pale reddish-brown speckles.

MARKED EGGS.—All our other birds lay eggs in some way marked. In dealing with these, one notes the existence of certain very definite family types. One egg for each of these will give an idea of these groups.

BLUE TIT

THE TIT TYPE.—Laid, with slight variations, by all the true Tits, the Willow Warbler, Wren, Nuthatch and Tree Creeper, and the Redbreast.

YELLOW HAMMER

THE BUNTING TYPE.—An egg marked with odd hieroglyphics, laid by the Yellow Hammer and all the other Buntings (except the Snow Bunting), the Hawfinch, Bearded Tit (marks minute) and often the Chaffinch and Guillemot. Other eggs which are often marked with

MAGPIE

SNIPE

QUAIL

hairlines, as well as other marks, may be classed with these :— Those of the Wagtails, Sedge Warbler, Goldfinch, Jay and Stone Curlew.

THE CROW TYPE.—The Crow family lay a greenish egg marked with a browner shade of the same colour. The Jay varies most from the type, her egg being yellower and paler. Most of the family are apt to vary much in the number and extent of the markings.

THE PLOVER TYPE.—This type of egg, recently so well-known to epicures, is common to a great many birds. The ground varies (often in the same species) from pale blue-green to dark brown, and the splashes vary in both number and blackness, but the type is common to the Stone Curlew, Woodcock (rounder), Snipe, and all the Waders, the Gulls, Terns and Skuas, and, in paler ground colours, to the Auks (except the Puffin). The Divers' eggs are usually darker in colour.

THE GAME BIRD MARKED TYPE.—This is usually a khaki

237

egg with distinctly red-brown markings, not grouped towards the big end, but dusted or evenly distributed. It belongs to the Rails, Red-Legged Partridge, Black Game and Capercaillie, Grouse, Ptarmigan and Quail. In the case of the last three, the markings are heavier and assume fantastic silhouette forms.

KESTREL

THE HAWK TYPE.—The Falcons and Kestrel lay eggs of which the plate is a type. The other birds of prey lay either white or bluish eggs (see *pp.* 235-6), or white eggs marked with a rich brown red of the same quality as that which colours the Falcons' eggs.

GOLDCREST

SHRIKE

THRUSH

NIGHTJAR

238

Among the remaining eggs one or two are easily recognized. The Puffin has a Duck's egg with both pale purple and brown spots, smeared with a wash of white ; the Thrush, a bright blue-green egg with small round black spots ; and the Nightjar's elliptical egg is yellowish with both pale purple and dark brown markings. The Shrike's egg, which varies in pale shades of ground colour, is usually belted with a crown of light reddish thorns. The Goldcrest's egg (smallest of all), though sometimes faintly spotted, is usually shaded rather than marked with a belt of grey or brown on creamy buff.

About those birds not yet named, it is harder to generalize, but the following notes may prove helpful :—

The Ground is White in the case of the Redbreast, all the Warblers, the Woodlark, the Swallow, the Crossbill, Greenfinch and Sparrows (sometimes bluish, see above *p.* 233).

The Ground is Blue or bluish-white, in the case of the other Finches, of the rest of the Thrush family, and the Water and White Wagtails.

The Ground is Yellow, or buff, for the Yellow and Grey Wagtails and the Spotted Flycatcher.

The Ground is obscured by the markings in the case of the Skylark and Pipits, and, to a lesser degree, the Woodlark. In a series of variable speckled-brown eggs, those of the Meadow Pipit are greyer, the Tree Pipit redder (see *p.* 233), the Rock Pipit browner, and the Skylark greener.

As to the *Markings*, these are usually :—

Red for the Mistle Thrush, Blackbird, Ring Ouzel, Stonechat, Redbreast, Snow Bunting, Chaffinch (dark) and, often, the Blackcap and Garden Warbler.

Chocolate or deep brown-red : Chiffchaff, Wood Warbler, Grasshopper Warbler (looks pinkish when the marks are minute and many), Woodlark, Bullfinch, Redpoll, Linnet and Twite (purplish), and Greenfinch, Siskin, Goldfinch, and Crossbill.

CHAFFINCH

Sandy : Whinchat, Sedge Warbler (often staining the whole egg), Grey and Yellow Wagtails and Spotted Flycatcher.

Green or greeny-brown : Whitethroat, Lesser Whitethroat, often the Blackcap and Garden Warbler, Dartford Warbler, Reed Warbler (often greening the whole egg), and Marsh Warbler.

Dark Brown : Water Wagtail, White Wagtail, Swallow, Hawfinch, and Tree Sparrow.

Many eggs are marked with two or more colours. The above notes refer only to the dominant shade.

INDEX

241

* NOTE.—In addition to the above there are certain obsolete sporting
terms which are worthy of record for their picturesqueness alone :
e.g., a *Herd* of Swans, a *Team*, *Sord*, *Sute* or *Badelynge* of Ducks,
a *Covert* of Coots, a *Muster* of Peacocks, a *Congregation* or *Wing*
of Plovers, a *Flight* of Doves, a *Dale* of Turkeys, a *Watch* of
Nightingales, a *Building* of Rooks, a *Murmuration* of Starlings, and
an *Exaltation* of Larks.

INDEX

245

INDEX

PRINTED IN GREAT BRITAIN BY THOS. FORMAN & SONS LTD., NOTTINGHAM